MW00611467

SCRIPTURALECTICS

SCRIPTURALECTICS

THE MANAGEMENT OF MEANING

VINCENT L. WIMBUSH

OXFORD
UNIVERSITY PRESS

OXFORD
UNIVERSITY PRESS

Oxford University Press is a department of the University of Oxford. It furthers
the University's objective of excellence in research, scholarship, and education
by publishing worldwide. Oxford is a registered trade mark of Oxford University
Press in the UK and certain other countries.

Published in the United States of America by Oxford University Press
198 Madison Avenue, New York, NY 10016, United States of America.

CIP data is on file at the Library of Congress
ISBN 978-0-19-066470-1

1 3 5 7 9 8 6 4 2
Printed by Sheridan Books, Inc., United States of America

for
Rosamond
Cary
Rodman

CONTENTS

PREFACE

This book is a transdisciplinary theoretical essay in the politics of language and communication. I engage such politics by problema-tizing and excavating what we in English shorthand continue to call "scriptures," first used to refer simply to "things written," the regis-tration of basic information (e.g., catalogs, lists, censuses, boundaries of properties, inventories of animals and slaves). Yet there was never a time before which (*quam anteriore tempore*) such registration of the "basic" was innocent of power relations. Having facilitated first the cataloging, stealing, and control of properties of all kinds (real estate, human bodies, and so forth), the mystification and ideological consolidation of empires (with their sacerdotal apparatuses), and then inspiring the invention and advancement of "religion" as separate but complexly overlapping domains and world-extensive social-cultural-political dynamics, phenomena, and orientation, the term "scriptures" in the modern world came to be associated almost exclusively with the center- and power-defining ("sacred") texts of "world religions." This narrowing of the valence of the term with the loss of the broad poi-gnant connections and deep sedimentation was a decisive development.

Fueled by awareness of its long captivity and apolitical flatten-ing by modernity's invention of "religion" as a separate apolitical domain, the initially broad and most expansive and politically charged use of the term "scriptures" is in this book reconsidered and rede-ployed: Scriptures are problematized and thereby made expansive again and excavated as texts (alone) to be not read but understood as discourse: as complex phenomena and dynamics; as mimetic rituals and practices; as ideologically charged orientations to and prescribed behaviors in the world; as structures of relationships and social formations (from small-scale traditional societies to complex extensive social-cultural associations, civilizations, empires, nation-states); as forms of communication and expressiveness (from various authoritative codes or doctrinal systems to vernacular performances). With such a term I am essentially naming and constructing a new transdisciplinary critical project about formation—turning around an expansive and radical (as in-depth) understanding of scriptures.

For myself I now insist on—and for others strongly encourage— the use as touchstones for framing, categorization, and analysis of the historical and ongoing experiences of the modern circum-Black Atlantic. Having been signified—that is, done violence to, specifically constructed to be freighted signs of and sites in the (d)evolution of the modern human, including human degradation, savagery, and otherworldliness, human (mis)re/cognition and (mis)communication—black peoples provide in the modern politics of language played *on* them (as slaves/objects), *with* them (as overdetermined signs), and eventually *by* them (as scripturalizing agents), wide and disturbing windows onto general critical conceptualization and analysis of the modern human.

With Chinua Achebe's novel *Things Fall Apart* as specific touchstone for this book, each chapter represents close reading and analysis of what is argued to be a representative or determinant moment or situation in the history of the formation of the Black Atlantic as part of a history of modern human consciousness and conscientization. Such a history, I argue, is reflected in the major turns in *scripturalectics*, part of the constructions of and orientations to the modern world, efforts to manage or control knowledge and/as meaning.

This book is part of a multiple-volume project on scriptures and culture as a critical project in historical social formation, using African diaspora experiences and expressivities and politics to think with. It follows and is supported by the argument I began to offer in *White Men's Magic: Scripturalization as Slavery*. I aim to follow this book with a third volume on the isolation, history, and analytics of the major turn identified in this book—rupture, the refusal of "scriptures" (as "white men's magic"). It is this refusal, this denial, this signifying (on scriptures)—*not* the projection of hyperreligiosity, including hyperfetishization of the Bible—that is poignant index of broad-based historical if not a defining African diaspora sensibility about and orientation to the world.

Vincent L. Wimbush
Founding Director
The Institute for Signifying Scriptures

INTRODUCTION

SCRIPTURALECTICS AS TURNS IN THE HUMAN QUEST FOR MEANING

With this book I introduce the concept of *scripturalectics* as an elaboration of, and framework and matrix for, my conceptualization of the phenomenon of *scripturalization*. Both fraught terms grow out of and aim to make more expansive and complex the popular usage and understanding of the English term "scriptures." I have staked much professional and intellectual and personal capital in arguing that the latter term begs deeper and wider analysis, cries out for excavation in light of its historically and perduring role as fraught abbreviation or mask that (un)veils much having to do with knowledge claims and collective consciousness or intelligence. In this respect, what scriptures have been made to do needs to be exploded, refracted, to be examined on terms befitting the complexity of the situation and dynamics partly viewed, partly obscured—far beyond the level of exegetical or lexical meanings, essentially upending the project of exegesis, or showing the latter to be imbricated in apologetics.[1] I maintain that what we mean by the term "scriptures" and by the dynamics associated with them at the most profound level point to the meta-lexical and meta-discursive, to the ultimate politics of language as part of the making and striving of the human, including humans' fears and anxieties about knowing or not knowing. Different types of fears and anxieties inspire and provoke scriptures, and scriptures are made to stoke and more broadly manage fears and anxieties.

In *White Men's Magic: Scripturalization as Slavery* (2012)[2] I argued, using Olaudah Equiano's signifying[3] on early modern Britain as

I

example, that *scripturalization* can and should serve as poignant shorthand for the meta-discursive regime and politics of language use, including speaking, writing, and reading and the accompanying claims about knowledge and collective intelligence and meaning that structure and determine nearly all the domains of communication and everyday aspects of modern life. Scripturalization has to do with the structure *of* meaning and meaning *as* structure.

The "texts" generally thought of as "religious" or "sacred" can now be considered for the purposes of the advancement of the theorizing that defines this book as historical, analytical and conceptual baseline, sources, fount, gateway (and so forth), as well as the most compelling and problematic metonymy for this phenomenon or set of dynamics—that is, for the politics of language, including meaning-making, meaning-translation, and meaning-management. But the former cannot and must not be thought of as exhausting the conceptualization and historical representations and expansive domains of the latter. Scripturalization is more expansive than—even as it includes—"religion." Certainly, scripturalization goes beyond "religion" as conceptualized and delimited and put in its sphere or domain by religion-allergic and -anxious "enlightened" figures.[4] It is beyond the modern Enlightenment-influenced ideological-cultural division between "sacred" and "secular." Notwithstanding significant differences that obtain in the modern world between and among human beings, what can be referred to as scripturalization *both* negotiates, perhaps even facilitates, structures, and exacerbates, such a division *and* ironically binds us together—into what Bourdieu calls the "universe of the undiscussed."[5] So scripturalization, I should like to argue, is the chief characteristic, the defining orientation, of such a universe, a textured and naturalized, wholly taken-for-granted semiosphere,[6] especially for moderns.

This book continues the discussion begun in *WMM* regarding scripturalization. As part of a critical historical reflection regarding how, by whom, and with what effects scripturalization is refracted in the world that most of my readers share with me, in this book I have turned back to some of those fraught moments and situations in the world that represent the "first contacts" between "civilization" and the "savage," the "West" and the "Other." This is the period in which scripturalization was most firmly constructed as a "reality" and consolidated as a regime—with much psychosocial, cultural, political, and other forms of violence and toxicity appertaining thereto. Following the poignant language used in Olaudah Equiano in his *Interesting Narrative* (1789),[7] and in an effort to make as plain as possible the process of construction and the reality of its consequences, I further labeled scripturalization "white men's magic." Given what is suggested by the general modern-language usage of the suffix "-ization"—consolidation; construction; regime—and given all that the terms "magic" and "white" differently but in juxtaposition uncomfortably and ironically and counterintuitively connote in the history of politics of the English language, by associating the terms I herewith place special focus on originary and ongoing social contexts of usage and the nature, potency, and politics and effects of the construction.

Although it does not have its original impetus in his work, my conceptualization of scripturalization is complimentary of and complementary to—and is in many respects an invited elaboration on—French theorist Michel de Certeau's notion of "scriptural economy" and of scriptural practice among the "everyday practices" that define social life. Advanced in his phenomenal book *The Practice of Everyday Life (L'invention du quotidien, vol. 1, Arts de Faire, 1980),*[8] his focus on the "scriptural" was provocatively pitched at the level of broad and general theorizing. But even as it was not without poignant examples here and there, the work clearly assumed modern-era and, most important, a racially and ethnically homogenous (viz., pan-white) Europe as singular if not supreme example and context (or, perhaps more accurately, with France as the most obviously practical focus). It seemed to assume that the European-inflected and -situated "everyday practices" reflected the universal experience or understanding. At any rate, I certainly read de Certeau's work as an invitation to probe further and more deeply into others' practices, problems, and contexts—historical and contemporary. As I made clear in WMM, and as I hope also to develop further in this and in forthcoming book projects, I have accepted the invitation and inspiration and challenge from a number of sources to contribute to, even help shape, the thinking and conversation about "scriptures" as shorthand for a set of everyday cultural practices that are reflective of complex social-cultural phenomena and dynamics, deeply imbricated in relations of power. That is, "scriptures" in *critical historical*[9] perspective represent a certain kind of cultural and psychosocial and political *work*—the set of social-cultural and politics consequences and effects—we sometimes wittingly but mostly unwittingly make do (for and to us), pointedly and ultimately in terms of (defending and opposing) the profound determinant that I continue here to term scripturalization.

Given my identity as (among other categories) African American/ black modern and my need to arrogate to myself the right to theorize expansively and creatively and freely with—not deny or psychically and conceptually run from—this identity; given the paucity of layered critical projects having to do with African Americans and black peoples throughout the world (not simply "Africentric" theological-exegetical apologetics in response to the mostly unacknowledged "white" traditional dominant theological-exegetical apologetics); given religion as an utterly complex and fascinating aspect of cultures in comparative terms; and, most important, given the analytical and theoretical possibilities black peoples generally provide as the persistent and chronic "strangers" and ex-centrics to and within scriptural civilizations or the modern world, I have decided (as already reflected in my use of Equiano's *Interesting Narrative*) that using black and black diaspora communities to think with about scriptural practices, their politics and social psychology and the like is for me instructive, compelling, freeing, provocative. Following the language and arguments set forth in Toni Morrison's now-famous provocative essay, I aim in this book to practice a type of criticism (among other types to be named below) that can be described as "playing in the dark." For such criticism the agenda and interests are neither "too polite [n]or too fearful" to take note of or embrace a "disrupting darkness."[10]

So following *WWM* and anticipating other further work on the history of the Black Atlantic's scripturalizing practices, this book is part of a multivolume project on scripturalization and the implications and ramifications attached therefrom and thereto. With Black Atlantic history as a focus and as an analytical and theorizing window, I attempt now to provide a broader accounting and analysis of scripturalization than was provided by my discussion of Equiano. The import of Equiano's "interesting narrative" was to draw attention to the phenomenon (of scripturalization) as "white men's magic"—from the point of view of the "stranger," the ex-centric. That such a perspective is important and needed is clear: It provides a concrete and limited, textured social context within which the phenomenon is made realistic, vivid, and dynamic. But critical study of this context requires that it be theorized in terms of historical-developmental and/or comparative perspective. In the end one of the most important contributions of Equiano's narrative is that it begs the basic question(s) that are otherwise normally occluded or denied within the world of dominants. Aspects of Equiano's story are so disturbing, so outrageous, that the reader (black or white and . . .) is forced either to turn away and disavow it or, as in my case, to wrestle with it and allow it to force a psychical and political reckoning, a tripping onto another level of questioning. The loudness, the flagrancy, the boldness of Equiano's play with scriptures—letting the reader see how the tricks are played—disturb and open up big questions and issues for consideration.

Scripturalization works best when and insofar as it is masked, as it appears to be something else—or when it escapes notice altogether. Equiano's questions in turn provide provocation and opportunity for me to raise questions about the longer history of the Black Atlantic and broader black diaspora scripturalizing, the terms of its participation in the regimes of scripturalization, and the complexities, the varied representations and types, forms, politics, and meanings of such participation. Equiano may in such a history be placed at or near the beginning of Black Atlantic scriptural engagement and practices; he may be argued to be a (pre-)figure(-ing) of a sort. What is clear is that he complexly belongs to, perhaps, as I have argued, can even be claimed to name the phenomenon of scripturalization and foreshadow if not figure Black Atlantic scripturalizing. Clearly, the (pre-)figure(-ing) and the foreshadowing suggest the need for further probing—of more complex and layered dynamics with evolutionary or at least imbricating stages of representation. These more psycho-social-cultural, discursive-expressive, historical-evolutionary, and recursive, overlapping dynamics I isolate and call here for the first time **scriptura*lectics*** (Greek: *lektos/n/on*; Latin: *legi-, leg-, ligi-, lig-, lect-, lex-, -lexia, -lexis, -lexic, -lectic*: read, readable; to choose words; to gather, collect; to pick out, choose; to read, recite), registering inflections, differences, or turns in meaning-making and communication. The term is apt insofar as it suggests layeredness, movement, with respect to discursive and social formation, the ultimate politics of language, even as it implies formation of the human.

That the self-understandings, practices and performances, politics and orientations of complexly minoritized communities in the United States and throughout the circum-Atlantic worlds have much to teach us about the complexly human should not startle or surprise. From their different forced positionalities on the margins, "minoritized"—what I prefer to call, following Charles Long, "signified"[11]—peoples open wide windows onto the challenges of human striving. This striving includes their experiences of pressures (even if never met) to conform to conventional-canonical construals of language, of forms of communication, representation, and embodiment (mimicry); opportunities to speak back to and confront and overturn conventionality (interruptions); and the need to experience ongoing meaningful relationships (orientation) to the centering orientation, politics, practices, and myths that define the modern.[12] It remains to be clarified how a project regarding scripture-reading as an example of everyday but nonetheless freighted human signifying practices might be conceptualized and carried out as a critical historical project.

In addition to the concept of scripturalization, another useful way of gaining a handle on what I argue here is to see this book as part of a major ongoing transdisciplinary research and writing project that I have conceptualized as an intellectual project in *critical comparative scriptures*.[13] Having affinities with other critical studies projects and discourses—critical legal, race, literary, historical studies, and the like—such a project involves the excavation of discourse and power, the ultimate politics of language, social formation, the making of the human, using scriptures/scripturalization as analytical wedge.

My modeling of the project in this particular book focuses mostly but not exclusively on the Anglophone Black Atlantic as portal, as the exemplum to think with. I use the poignant English abbreviation "scriptures" as handle for the project. Again, the term as I use it here is at once basic (having to do with things written, texts) and elastic and weighty (having to do with regimes of language, discourse, all forms of communication and knowledges). It certainly includes phenomena and dynamics that, since the pressures and influences of the Enlightenment, pertain to and delimit "religion," but I see associated with it so much more: Insofar as the project involves problematizing "scriptures" as cross-cultural phenomenon, I do not ask—as might the tribal theologian or conserv(e)-ative court/legal scholar or civil-nationalist philologist or historical critic—what is the fixed and true content-meaning (or historical background or literary-rhetorical construction) of this or that representation of scriptures. As a scholar of what Pierre Nora calls *critical history* (and culture), I ask instead: What is the meaning of inventing, and then making assumptions and claims (about knowledge and authority) in connection with, scriptures? What work do we make scriptures do for us—and to us? What cultural practices are involved? What power dynamics and issues are imbricated and structured and codified, and sometimes questioned and resisted, in connection with such practices? What fears and anxieties motor the practices and manage the resultant system? Given this set of questions and issues, scripturalization can be understood to be one of the most important historical and ongoing phenomena, effects, and consequences that can be isolated in a critical comparative scriptures project and in critical formation discourse.

There has been no critical work of exactly the sort (viz., with the combination of focus, critical orientation, and transdisciplinarity) I aim to model with this book. I understand this book in its orientation, if not in its focus on specific text-content or historical context, to

7

be plowing new ground, essentially *inventing and modeling a critical field of research and inquiry*. It should occasion no shock or surprise that European Enlightenment–inspired modern-world theological/ religious scholarship, including biblical scholarship that over the decades developed as a subset discourse with its own set of issues and politics, has with all its pretensions to being "enlightened" and "secular" and "critical," been consistently and forthrightly none of these in terms of interests, agenda, and orientation: The practices of historical criticism (and related newer forms of criticism of biblical studies and in all the fields of theological studies as umbrella category) have, it needs to be said, reconstructed ancient worlds and ancient truths that seem remarkably reflective and affirming, even naturalizing/ codifying, of modern white men's worlds—that is, European or Euro-American worlds.

More surprisingly, scholarship on African Americans and on the African diaspora more broadly has not paid a great deal of serious attention to the "religious" textures and gestures and performances and practices of such populations. When there has not been neglect altogether among scholars in fields and disciplines outside theology and religious studies, there is evidence aplenty of grudging and awkward chagrined gestures or nods toward or a puzzling and flat overdetermination regarding "religion" among black folks. There has been among scholars of all fields and disciplines far too much of the uncritical acceptance of a set of assumptions about black peoples' simple and persistent hyper-religious sensibilities and practices. And there has been either hyper-romanticization or hyperventilation (in other words, flatness of analysis and narrowness of perspectives) regarding "the black church," but little or certainly not enough of that which is deserved and needed—complex and layered theorizing about how Black Atlantic peoples have invented and used "religion" and how they have "per-formed" the religious, as well as how "religion" and religious forms and practices and discourses have affected and been used to (re)orient Black Atlantic peoples. Whatever the reasons, "black religion" remains woefully undertheorized. We are in my view still a great distance from understanding the "work" "religion" was made to do among the folk who were part of the Black circum-Atlantic worlds.[14]

Scholarship on African American and African diaspora religious history—of whatever style or subfield or orientation—has certainly not placed focus exactly on the point I am pressing here. To be sure, some attention has been paid to African Americans' reading of the Bible here and there. But these works have been quite general and have subsumed this phenomenon under some other interests (e.g., slave religion, ideology of the civil rights movement, the construction of black piety, and so forth) without problematization of what "Bible" signifies in larger historical and comparative social-cultural and political terms.

And even the still-small-but-growing numbers of black scholars of the Bible have not changed the situation, from my point of view. Even black biblical scholars on the whole are ironically and puzzlingly and shockingly still locked into the general guild's syndrome—registering fetishism of the texts in the orientation to exegesis of texts as the bottom line agenda. Still persistent among persons of color within this guild is not only the orientation to exegesis but the taking on of the burden to find special (black) content-meaning, the assumed belated right or liberating reading, or the "recovery" of an earlier, more genuine liberating "black" reading of this or that unproblematized "text" or a black biblical-mythical figure. Whether for the sake of recovery, oppositional, subcultural stances, or celebratory politics, the agenda continues for the most part, in spite of historical ironies, to be the black- (or Asian-, or Latino\a-)inflected (historical- or literary-critical) explication of "the text."[15]

That such agendas are problematic has been my argument and the focus of my thinking for the past three decades or more. What black folks' *uses* of the Bible—and other scriptures—may mean for the very understanding of the phenomenon of modern scripturalizing and of modern black formation as a part of the larger phenomenon has not been given the attention it needs—indeed, it has barely been recognized as important. Such a focus represents a different type of critical (and political) orientation and project. There have been few fellow travelers along the way.[16]

9

I have tried to model this different type of critical project using African Americans to think with—thus, the project I conceptualized in the 1990s called African Americans *and* the Bible (or scriptures more generally). The conjuncture is key here: It suggests orientation not to exegesis, or the black-inflected or interested meaning of or in the text, but to the meaning of the complex engagements and *uses* of "texts" on the part of a diverse people in an expansive history of fraught representations, performances, social-cultural-political efforts, gestures, reactions, and interests. Preoccupation with exegesis, I have maintained for most of my professional career, generally has historically reflected a stable or at least thick-limned if not "happy"[17] social world in which the lexical-philological-cultural-theological engagement of fairly settled center-forming texts represents sophisticated social-cultural-nationalist mirroring and the possibility of imagining and realizing stable *meaning* as projection of advancement and dominance. The interest in reaching some clear stable/final correct meaning of the texts is correlative of dominant social and political station. Such interest and practice are not and never have been practical for—hardly ever to the advantage of—black folks treated as "strangers" or aliens within the discursive worlds as drawn up.

Yet, as I indicated above, many if not most black students of the Bible strangely persist in the agenda of black-inflected exegesis. As strange and as confounding as it may be, this persistence is somewhat understandable: In the biblical/scriptural formation that is the United States, it is difficult to resist playing the same game that marks ongoing cultural formation and discourse. Mimetics in that key is surely evidence of the long and ongoing heart-tugging struggle on the part of "strangers" to build a "home" and belong—in personal, social, including professional terms. I would add here that this persistent and unchecked or nonreflexive mimetics is unfortunate, even dangerous. And educated clerics and academic scholars reflect this struggle and fall into the trap no less—perhaps even more so—than others. As the rich signifying tradition in black culture has made evident, there is no mimetics quite like that of the educated marginal. (On this point W. E. B. Du Bois, Zora Neale Hurston, and Ralph

Ellison have been instructive.) This situation is nonetheless problematic because at this point in a long enough history of tortured black exegetical mimetics—academic and/or popular—and all that it represents in terms of "white men's magic," it is ironic and ultimately self-defeating, a dead end, a game black folk cannot win. Ishmael Reed is right in arguing that there is a need for black folks to re-dis-cover their own "texts";[18] but I should like to add that they need also their own situation-appropriate and compelling interpretive practices and, as much as possible, self-reflexivity—that is, a sense of the self-serving or -affirming politics involved. The few scholarly projects that are by self-description and advertisement focused on the history of engagements or uses of the Bible have not been expansive enough in either conceptualization or coverage or both. They have tended not to address the matter of how the black engagements of the Bible represent and refract the broader historical comparative cultural formation of the "Black Atlantic"/"Black diaspora" on the one hand and "the Bible"/"scriptures" as cultural phenomenon on the other.[19] This is not unimportant in terms of positioning black peoples—in Africa and throughout the African diasporas—and the Bible as scriptures, complexly within modernity. Particular figures and communities have been given some attention in projects but have generally not been placed within the larger critical framework focused on (critical comparative) scriptures that I hope to introduce and advance in this book.

One of the underlying critical ideological and theoretical-analytical principles of this book is that "Black Atlantic"/"African diaspora" and "Bible"/"scriptures" as categories should be analyzed in complex inter-relationship and in terms of critical cultural historical and comparative analysis—as analytic windows for each other. None of the categories is to be accepted at face or for rhetorical/literary value; each is to be excavated in order to determine its functions in relationship to others, within and against different historical frameworks and contexts. By analytically pressing "Black Atlantic"/"African diaspora" against "Bible"/"scriptures" I hope not only to deconstruct each, but also to have the one lift the other into different (if not larger) contexts, timeframes, spheres, arenas, domains, critical frameworks, and questions that define the modern.

Coming to this point of critical orientation around scriptures is for many reasons very difficult. The stumbling blocks in the way of the needed socio-psychological, social-cultural-political, and intellectual journeying are many and are quite daunting. Scriptures, like all social-cultural constructions, are most powerful the extent to which they control the nature of inquiry about them and the order of mimetics in relationship to them.[20] An attempt at providing testimony about my own journeying and escape (back) into the "underground" or ex-centric space is in order—if not for my soul and orientation, at least for the readers' perspective.

My coming to the construal of the critical comparative scriptures intellectual project is a long history of professional-intellectual and personal risk-taking, struggle, development, growth, learning. I began my academic career in the early 1980s by trying to be the best possible historical critic—with focus on the Christian Bible—I could be. How came I to this discursive field and its play? The short answer for the agenda of this chapter in this book is that I wanted to understand the performances and practices, the sounds and rituals that marked my little world (which was home and the environs of lower-middle class black protestant culture) and—as I came to appreciate—the circles of larger worlds (which included the southeastern part of the Bible Belt; the United States as biblical/scriptural formation, insofar as it was wearing the rest of the scriptural garb befitting a scriptural formation; and, of course, even that larger determining world—the Christianized scripturalized West). Although without the language and concepts to come to full expression at the time, as I look back on the period of my youth and early adulthood that included the years of graduate study, I recall feeling that I needed to understand some things, why things were as they were in terms of scriptural rhetorics and practices and politics and how they impinged on and determined/signified/(en-)scripturalized me. I had at the time no clear concepts, no language for expression, only a vague feeling, a sensibility about, the questions and issues I needed to address. How come this play and politics with scriptures that marked my little world and the larger world? How came my people to such play, and with what historical and ongoing consequences? At any rate, these questions and issues pointedly, poignantly, and ironically did not meet the authorized interests, orientation, and agenda of the academic fields and discourses where I eventually found myself. The problematics of the uses of the Bible were not thought to belong to a study of the Bible program! The most important lesson I was taught was to *police* myself around such issues. I was thrown onto myself. I made myself silent, oftentimes a stutterer. The books—including the supposed feigned apolitical, but really conservative discourse that determined what they meant in academic-political terms and how they were to be engaged and deployed—did not speak to me. I was, as Equiano would put it, a "stranger."

Notwithstanding this feeling of being a "stranger," I do not pretend even in this season of my life to be able to fully and honestly fathom how or why I persisted (pride? tenacity?), pretty much alone—that is, without mentors and colleagues who could understand and help me navigate the way with my issues. I advanced along a fairly standard and undistinguished track in graduate studies.[21] But after having taken the doctoral degree, having made it clear to myself and to others that a ministerial career was not in the offing for me, I threw myself into an academic career in Christian scriptures. Going this route meant orienting myself to the discourses shaped around an invented (thin slice of) "antiquity"—Greco-Roman, early Christian, late antiquity, and so forth. Such discourses were invested in the unacknowledged politics and practices—highly intellectualized, mind you, with obfuscation thick and piled high—of apologetics of the modern dominant religious, cultural, and nationalistic regimes, with their investments in inventing and managing discourses about biblical and related antiquities. I now see more clearly that I was trained—as biblical exegete/historical critic—to be a good ideological "civil servant," tradent, interpreter of, apologist for, the Western regime that was centered around but extended far beyond "religion" and "the book," as these had come to be understood in the narrowest post-Enlightenment terms of modern-era high-protestant-inflected ascetical piety, intellectualism, and civility.

Of course, my field is not the only one that functions in this way; almost all the traditional Western world humanities fields are so constructed and oriented. Yet there is something quite poignant about being in a field that loans to the others the very terms (canon, scriptures, Bible, commentary, hermeneutics, exegesis) by which the chief interests and politics of the regime (construction and closure) are practiced and (mis-) identified. So there is a sense in which the baselines (and vocabulary) of local and translocal regime construction and maintenance—historical and contemporary—are appropriately and compellingly found and named in what I term scripturalization.

Slowly but steadily evolving or turning away from such theologically inflected and/or historicist orientation; or, even more accurately and pointedly, as historian of religion Charles Long might in his inimitable manner put it, "crawling back" to myself and to that world that nurtured me—because after reading Du Bois we have come to recognize that survival and "striving" in the West resulted in, perhaps required, the black self to be split, doubled, disavowed—I sought to navigate differently. Given my professional situation, and without more experienced mentors and friends and colleagues in the field to help, I strove and crawled as best I could.

It was the transdisciplinary and collaborative project on African Americans and the Bible (AFAMBIB) that I conceptualized and directed in New York City at Union Theological Seminary from 1996 to 2003 that first represented self-arrogation of a degree of real academic-intellectual and professional freedom. But it also signified to some observers and academic colleagues near and far a type of intellectual and academic, social-cultural, and religious perfidy. I began hearing about some colleagues' anxiety about what I was up to: for some I seemed to be going off the academic rails, veering into strange territory. A few colleagues whispered to me about the whispers about my having left the field.

At the time I created the AFAMBIB project in the 1990s, I was identified as a faculty member in what was considered by protestant tradition the touchstone field, the Biblical Field, located in one of the last bastions of self-ascribed "mainline"—protestant—religion, long on its last legs, roiling to survive and to define itself in a post-mainline world. This was Union Theological Seminary in the City of New York, as it likes to identify itself. Being black and in that field at Union was unprecedented and was in that decade viewed by most as noteworthy, an ironic sign of belated and twisted progressivism. After so much noise made by students about the absence of faculty of color in that field, I was as a black faculty member, welcomed and embraced—by most members of that community. It was assumed that with my credentials I had been sufficiently socialized into the politics of the white-mainline-protestant orientation to the Bible. Had I been so oriented, I suspect the quest to find (black-affirming) black characters *in* the Bible would have been deemed an acceptable or tolerated project, complementing the orientation of black liberation theology and befitting what remained of the protestant-inflected religio-modernist paradigm (even if such a quest was marginalized within some circles of what was left of respectable intellectualist protestantism). After all, there could never be found enough black characters to disturb the white Bible. In addition, ultimately, in spite of individual and subgroup tastes, such a project did indeed fit (and was determined and conditioned by) the traditional historicist/theological paradigm.

What proved unsettling—at Union and elsewhere across intellectual protestant-land—was the project I conceptualized and advanced. This project included the freighted and provocative conjunction *"and"* that betokened something different from the normally assumed preposition *"in"* and the attendant historicist-theological orientation, and so it was not so welcome. It did not fit. I had begun through my ascetics of "crawling back" to an integrated and free-thinking, free-speaking self to notice more clearly the larger ideological structural framework and regime—unnamed at the time, but presaging what I now call scripturalization—that determined the African American rapprochement with the Bible. This discovery brought with it potential for understanding differently the whole enterprise of scripture-making and scripture uses. It was essentially a type of intellectual marronage, an escape from the field that primarily held together the statist protestant-inflected paradigm and ideological regime.[22]

The AFAMBIB project ended its first phase with a large conference in 1999 that modeled what I would later come to think of as the beginning of the different orientation to research on African Americans (with sensitivity to, but clearly not enough representation of, black folks throughout the circum-Atlantic—Africa, the Caribbean, and Central and South America, and beyond). This different orientation entailed focus on African Americans (as freighted subset of the Black Atlantic if not the entire black diaspora) and the Bible (as fraught metonymy for "scriptures"—in varied types of representations, not merely texts—of all cultures). Whether I made the case then in terms clearly and pointedly enough I am not sure, but I had in mind nothing less than making use of the one complex category—African Americans—for theorizing about the other category—"the Bible." And vice versa. And there was the not fully articulated hope at the time that the two categories analyzed in conjuncture would open a window onto the complexity of the human.

As part of the opening keynote event of the 1999 AFAMBIB conference (which concluded the multiple-year project) I presented an address that was also included (in revised and expanded form) as the introductory essay for the published collection of conference presentations (*African Americans and the Bible: Sacred Texts and Social Textures*, 2000, 2001).[23] Entitled "Reading Darkness, Reading Scriptures," this essay represents my first sustained attempt to problematize and theorize the conjuncture of African Americans and the Bible (and all that pertained to these categories). Along with a short popular essay, *The Bible and African Americans: A Brief History* (2003),[24] the "Reading Darkness" essay represented for me no turning away from the crawling back.[25] And in the aftermath of the writing of this essay, an experience I liken to that of Richard Wright's character in "The Man Who Lived Underground,"[26] an experience of a kind of intellectual going underground, even at points when, out of whatever circumstances or concessions or constraints, the academic disciplinary "overground" (this term also draws on and anticipates my engagement of Richard Wright and his provocative novella) has been revisited (in terms of engaging in some fairly traditional academic practices as far as my field is concerned), it has nonetheless been experienced and seen, with significant implications and ramifications, through *dark-ened* glasses. Since the AFAMBIB project, I have not been the same academic-intellectual or human being.

I am with these questions in agreement with literary critic Srinivas Aravamudan in his important challenge that we put focus on "tropicopolitans" and their tropicopolizations—that is, how subalterns "read" and "make do (*fait faire*)" with the dominant world, and less how they read the content-meaning of texts/scriptures of empire. Aravamudan was with such an orientation following the performances and accepting the challenges of those tropicopolitans such as Olaudah Equiano, the focus of a chapter in his book *Tropicopolitans: Colonialism and Agency, 1688–1804* (1999).[27] I argued in *WMM* that Equiano read not (merely) the (lexical-meaning of the) English scriptures, but the scripturalizing practices of the English elite who as inventors and wielders of their texts exercised *"unbounded influence over the credulity and superstition of the people."* It was just such "influence" or "magic," that was understood by Equiano to function much like the "magic" that he imagined[28] had obtained among the Igbo "priests" and "magicians."

The larger context of Equiano's reading of the English will be useful: The first chapter of Equiano's narrative was devoted to introducing the (European) reader to "my countrymen," "a nation of dancers, musicians, and poets," and "our manner of living." This introduction was done not for the sake of documenting the facts about his folks, but in the interest of convincing his readers that, with few minor differences in style and with a concession that the one group had in some respects developed much more than the other, "Eboan Africans" and Europeans are similar—"the one people had sprung from the other," perhaps; most certainly, because God "hath made of one blood all nations." It is this interest in establishing similarity that governs or frames Equiano's reference to Igbo traditions of "public worship" and "priests"(and all that pertains to such)—language that already betrays on what terms the description and judgment are made:

> Though we had no places of public worship, we had priests and magicians, or wise men ... They calculated our time, and foretold events, as their name imported, for we called them *Ah-affoe-way-cah*, which signifies calculators or yearly men ...
>
> These magicians were also our doctors or physicians. They practice bleeding by cupping, and were very successful in healing wounds and expelling poisons. They had likewise some extraordinary method of discovering jealousy, theft, and poisoning; they success of which no doubt they derived from their *unbounded influence* over the credulity and superstition of the people ... (*Interesting Narrative*, 42; his emphases)

This turn of phrase and twist of language about "influence" in Equiano has disturbed me for some time. The language is problematic—at once too easy and hard to fathom; both apt and incongruent; both familiar and odd: Who speaks this way, in what contexts, and to what end? Although I grant that the whole point of Equiano's narrative was to demonstrate that he could "talk that talk," could make the book "speak," could make himself into an Englishman, in seeking as he does in his Chapter 1 to draw a parallel between white men's ways and the ways of the Igbo, he overreaches. He presses his ethnic-tribal-cultural ecumenism and religious comparativism too hard. "Unbounded influence" is the language and ideology not of any local tribe or village, Igbo or otherwise. It is the language and ideology of the "world religion," or of a "scriptural economy" and the extensive civilization or empire or nation that it may inspire and help construct and naturalize. "Unbounded influence" seems out of step with the textures of life in the scale of social organization that was the real or imagined Igboland. Equiano's descriptor applied to his tribesmen smacks of an understandable desperation of sorts to compare favorably the scriptural societies of the sort that was late-eighteenth-century Britain to the (imagined) world of the Igbo. With such comparison he rhetorically positioned himself to be given serious consideration, if not total acceptance, among white men.

But this problem of misapplication raises important issues and questions that I had not more fully considered before. What is further begged is the question not so much what relationship Equiano wanted to obtain between the world of the British and the Igbo—he makes it clear that because the ways of white men were dominant and authorized, he aims with his narrative to perform and assume whiteness—but the relationship that likely actually obtained. Who mimics whom? And that question in turn begs another: Given what is known about ways of knowing and patterns of authority in tribal and village societies throughout the world, if Igbo "priests" and "magicians" were very unlikely to have been thought to possess unchecked authority, then what does his thinking here suggest about the relationship between European and African local indigenous worlds and their construals of knowing and authority, discourse and power, the politics of language? If Equiano's point of comparison is unsurprisingly, even compellingly, fictional, what reality does it nonetheless reflect? And what deep issues—about human consciousness and relations—are reflected in such comparison?

Here is how the concept of scripturalization, the project of signifying (on) scriptures/critical comparative scriptures, and the argument in this book for scripturalectics as handle for reading evolutionary and refractionary dynamics come into play and focus. The most profound challenge of Equiano's narrative is to help the reader see the reality of white men's magic in terms of scripturalization and as part of the general dynamics of scripturalectics. I suggest that Equiano's narrative reflects and provokes further questioning about scripturalization as dominant and extensive construction that now requires critical investigation, negotiation, and engagement. It is, as Equiano makes clear, the discursive/ideological playing field onto which we all are now more or less forced. It has a wide if not global reach; in terms of both claims and arguable near-reality it is—not the local Igbo priests and wise men—of "unbounded influence." We have in Equiano's narrative a window onto the demands, the violence—the always potential if not actual slavery?[29]—such a construction makes of Equiano, and through him, not only all black "strangers," but all who live within scriptural civilizations. We must ask—as his narrative provokes us to ask—how did it come to be so? How did white men's magic that is scripturalization come to be? What prefigured it? What follows it or is influenced or determined by it? What motors it? Sustains it? What are the consequences of being pulled into it, being determined by it, being forced to negotiate life on its terms?

This book is an attempt to address these questions—about the ultimate politics of language and about the fears and anxieties underlying and motoring it. As is already evident in my discussion of Equiano above and in the close reading in WMM, I make this attempt by making use of, or situating the phenomenon in relationship to, a segment of the history of practices and experiences of the Black Atlantic. I should like in this book to try to account for scripturalization as white men's magic—a reflection of whiteness as privilege—as the dominant and extensive regime of language use and authorized forms of knowing, and such a regime as it were in the middle of the story or as part of a complex development of stages of near=global historical human systems of knowing. I should like to do this by exploring how such a regime developed not in isolation or as bloodless abstraction, but in relationship to other/prior dynamic and pulsating ways of knowing and being, and how and to what ends other types of responses to, and reiterations and instantiations of, it later developed.

But in connection with and emerging out of scripturalization as phenomenon reflective of whiteness as ideological-political orientation and the baseline on which dominant "standard" discourse rests—including in some ironic complex and unavoidable respects the features of the project that is this book!—three types of *reading formations*,[30] types of systems of language use, knowledge claims, stages in the structures of consciousness or meaning and orientations to the world, including the fear and anxieties that mark these orientations, will be isolated and analyzed as scripturalectics: (1) local cultures' totalistic forms of knowledge/ways of knowing, organized around ritual play, or mask-ing; (2) extensive societies and their claims to totalistic-universal knowledge/way of knowing, or meaning transcendent reflected in their invention and advancement of the scriptural; and (3) ex-centrics' or humiliated peoples' mimetics/interruptions/interrogations of the extensive-totalistic-universal and its orientations and politics—signifying (on) scriptures—and their embracing of ideological-psychical marronage, resulting in the radical degrading of meaning.

The second formation is scripturalization. This book is opportunity to explore it more deeply and broadly. It stands for the still determinative formation, with the risk of enslavement of all—to varying degrees, in different respects—to it or within it always possible, always threatening. It is that which, in terms of the British iteration or representation, Equiano confronted, performed, and tried to signify on.

The first formation—a "reading" formation in the appropriately expansive and capacious sense of the term, notwithstanding its association with oral and local cultures—will be considered not simply as chronologically *prior* and psychosocially anachronistic to the dominant reading that is scripturalization; it is a baseline, whence we all developed; it is also complexly perduring in our time, dislocated and muted, carried and translated by the outliers, the subaltern, and denied by all others. It cannot now be "recovered" in any simple manner. It need not be reached for in nostalgic or apologetic terms. It reflects basic fears and anxieties. Yet it may provide possibilities for turning back onto, checking and challenging and denaturalizing, the second long-dominant formation that is scripturalization.

The third formation—associated with the disruption that is voice-finding and the agency conscientization among the humiliated represents—will be discussed in terms of its reflection of the ongoing reiterations and construals of scripturalization as well as possibilities for moving beyond it, in marronage, in a state in which meaning fades and marks and locates, liberates from, but also forces the engagement of basic fear.

These three turns in and types of formation should not be understood to be chronologically successive or to represent mutually exclusive temporalities; they overlap in time and in all but the earliest barely recoverable historical situations (e.g., before the onset and fairly widespread popular practices of modern-world writing and reading). Insofar as these formations represent forms or structures of consciousness and social psychologies and orientations, they are more than ideas about ideas, concepts about concepts, or abstract abstractions. I also understand them to be more fundamentally social textures and psychosocial dynamics, orientations of the embodied, everyday practices of ordinary lives that are scripted, made meaningful. So analysis of these formations of knowing, of "readings" and "writings," requires where possible radical transdisciplinary excavation—of social-cultural practices, psychosocial orientations, rhetorical-discursive expressivities, meta-rhetorical-discursive representations, and the political. With such approaches, and using ways and regimes of knowing as wedge—and scriptures as shorthand for such—the agenda is to help explain further and I think more provocatively how human beings have been and continue to be constructed, and with what consequences.

Given this agenda of isolating and probing the three writing–reading formations, and in light of the analytical power that close reading of Equiano's narrative—in the ex-centric perspective of the black "stranger"—provided me in my previous book as a window onto the larger meta-lexical dynamics and phenomenon of scripturalization—in this book I also make use of a powerful modern-world text as springboard. Whereas Equiano's narrative took a snapshot of the formation that is mid- to late-eighteenth-century British-inflected scripturalization, Chinua Achebe's oeuvre of fiction affords the opportunity and challenge to consider not only a later period in history (with some focus on or around if not within Igboland) but also a longer arc or trajectory of contact, influence, movement, and imbrication, among other issues, between blacks and whites that resulted in among things the construction of the Black Atlantic. And, of course, as an artist, Achebe's representation is even more textured and complex. More to the point and poignancy, Equiano led me to Achebe because they together represent the perspective gained through continued focus on the experiences of the black "stranger"—from Equiano's experiences away from "home" (and mostly) in Britain to the experiences of those at home for whom colonization has made "things fall apart," those who made to be "no longer at ease," no longer "at home," those who were sold and stolen away and would need over the centuries to construct identity and "home" in exile and marronage throughout the Atlantic world (and beyond). Insofar as it seems to assume the sort of challenge faced by Equiano and to anticipate the sort of challenge to be (continuously) faced by those sold and stolen away, Achebe's work is powerfully positioned to facilitate critical thinking about the history of the Black Atlantic in terms of a history of regimes of knowing as a history of human-making.

So it is important to make clear that my interest in Achebe's work has to do ultimately not with its use as (dehistoricized/depoliticized) art or as source of history. It is in fascinating terms, like Equiano's story, part performance and history. Again, like my engagement of Equiano, I intend in this book to read Achebe's famously historical fiction as narrative worlds into which I am moved and inspired and provoked to raise questions and issues, analyze problems and situations, even imagine scenarios and dynamics that standard historiography or standard literary criticism may ignore. The narrative worlds that Achebe opens to the reader are precisely those in which the pertinent dynamics occur(red) in realistic historical periods and frames—vibrant, realistic, almost all critics have called them. But Achebe is critical for me not because he simply records the past, not because he simply invents pasts, but because he narrates worlds that recall and reanimate a particular (construal of the) past—for the sake of facilitating a view of and orientation to the present and to the future. He is significant for my purposes less because he can be claimed to have gotten everything historically or historiographically "right" than because he helps me and all readers consider what may be the most important problematic—the challenge (even tragedy) that lies in the regime that informs and structures, limits and overdetermines, our present consciousness and knowing. Brilliantly charting the course of the challenges—having to do with ways of knowing and human-making—and some responses to them through the experiences of the peoples he knew best and cared about most remains Achebe's powerful legacy.

So the baseline and running text throughout this book is Chinua Achebe's now universally acclaimed novel *Things Fall Apart* (hereafter *TFA*). I make use as of it as the primary or springboard text-source for analysis of all three moments or turns or inflections in scripturalectics.[31] This work I find most compelling as a narratological argument for and a window onto the different types of consciousness and orientations that help explain the end-of-the-nineteenth-turn-into-the-twentieth-century people about whom Achebe writes. It is all the more poignant that such people are dark peoples, Igbos, Africans, with all that the times—the period of the height of European arrogance and hegemony in Africa mask-ing as colonial "donation"—and these names signify. *TFA* I read closely but in complex ways—in some respects far differently from the way Achebe and some professional literary critics imagined; in some other respects I would read and argue along lines provocatively close to his interests and agenda. My reading is unique and I think compelling. I interpret *TFA* in this book to think with and to think about the formations of (and the challenges to) black peoples in the modern world, their imagination, consciousness and conscientization, their orientation and agency, their meaning-making and structures and communication of meaning. The turns or stages in these dynamics—especially because they take place *after* Gutenberg, *after* the invention and consolidation of "world religions" as scriptural formations and their incorporation in and parallels to the (re-)formations of modern nations—I identify as scripturalectics. The three different types and turns and moments of scripturalectics—sketched above—I read into and see threaded through *TFA*; they are about humans' quest to know and to mean. These isolated types and turns in scripturalectics provide the structure of chapter divisions for the book.

Framed by this orienting introductory chapter and a summary conclusion that will suggest next steps in the analysis and discussion, this book is tightly organized around the isolation and analysis of knowing–writing–reading formations found in or implied by *TFA*. These formations are also orientations to and forms of consciousness about the (collective) self and the world, or constructions of systems of meaning. So we are brought to the following sketch for the book:

Chapter 1, "*Aru Oyim De De De Dei!*": Mask-ing Meaning, is focused on the narratological picture of the regular but rich rhythms and textures that is painted of life in the village of Umuofia in *TFA*. I make use of this "painting" in order to outline what are among the most important aspects of what is according to my schema the most basic and baseline human orientation to the world and its protocol for seeking and finding meaning that persisted into the modern era. Such an orientation involves a system of knowing that is tied to place and the mask-ing rituals that define and mark and make compelling place or location.

Chapter 2, "Pacification of the Primitive Tribes": Meaning as White Savagery, focuses on the evidence in *TFA* for the formation and orientation that represents the regime of knowledge, its politics of language, its effects on discourse and power that is (named by me as) scripturalization. Also heretofore labeled by me as part of the study of Equiano's narrative about his life "white men's magic," it is associated with the coming of the white men to the Umuofia in *TFA* and the falling apart of all things. I argue that the invasion is most pointedly regime change— from the traditional world and its epistemics that defined the village to the regime and its system of knowing and meaning-making and representation that is associated with the European invaders and their claims to superior forms of knowing. With its turn from the textures of village life to the village's inscription and its permanent and fixed and authoritative representation in the book planned by the district commissioner, *TFA* poignantly captures the tragedy in such a turn.

Chapter 3, "We Have Fallen Apart": The Rupture of Meaning, focuses on the ramifications of the regime of scripturalization for those who by its violent inscription and politics are made "strangers," made to "fall apart," made "no longer at ease." From within the prison houses of the regime, and against the backdrop of the collapse of tradition, some Umuofians escape—in different respects and terms. Some join the religion and bureaucratic systems of the white men. Others literally do battle. And others still opt for any number of ways in between. The point to be made is that this turn represents the explosion and degradation of meaning. I do not and need not argue this turn as the only or definitive one for the Black Atlantic. It is enough for me to identify and isolate it and argue for it as significant historical orientation.

A summary conclusion takes up the matter of the significance of the discussion in terms of what critical and analytical windows focused on the Black Atlantic open up and addresses some ongoing issues and problems that require attention. An argument for more research and analysis of Black Atlantic formation of collective intelligence and what more this may contribute to analysis of the human is made. I shall here always take opportunity to revisit the argument about what this essay implies about the orientation of critical studies in scriptures.

CHAPTER 1

"ARU OYIM DE DE DE DEI!"

MASK-ING MEANING

And when ... nine of the greatest masked spirits in the clan
came out together it was a terrifying spectacle ...
—*Things Fall Apart, Chapter 1*

It is a story that grips. It paints such rich colors and affords the reader access to amazingly deep social texture. The proverbs are gripping. The characters' discourses and actions are arresting. The storyline and development are compelling—they are full of drama, comedy, pathos, transcendence, tragedy. Readers can hardly help laughing, crying, feeling anger, sighing, dancing. What else is there? What more can one expect or find? In short, *TFA* as novel is compelling, fascinating; it is for me, as a son of the African diaspora and student of its cultural traditions, rich, complexly woven, and rather astounding. Astounding that through this story I am taken on each occasion of reading it on a journey as inspiring as it is unsettling, not unlike the experience I had of traveling to the west African coast to see here and there representations and iterations of authentic and layered African life as well as ghosts at those points where ensnared and enslaved natives were forced to go through doors and experiences of "no return." Not unlike the experience Saidiya Hartman[1] reported having had on her journey to Ghana, my own journeying there a few years ago and my own reading of *TFA* take me on a similar journey—in this case on a narratologically induced psychic, but no less disturbing, journey. It takes me on a fraught journey—from the situation of the rich, as in realistic and complex, not at all nostalgic or utopic, village life with its own rhythms and sensibilities and orientations and integrity and problems to the point that I myself came to see firsthand "things falling apart," that is, the continuing twenty-first century consequences and effects of the colonial order. This stressed endpoint of the novel remains for me a poignant one and a touchstone for the conceptualization and structuring of this book: It is the point in the story at which a colonial "administrator" becomes a "student of primitive customs" and as such begins to *inscribe* the people of the village into (his dominant white world's version of) colonial history. So *TFA* as novel both anticipates and ends and projects forward with the violence that is the signification that is *The Pacification of the Primitive Tribes of the Lower Niger*.

The frontispiece to the 1724 edition of missionary and ethnologist Joseph-Francois Lafitau's *Moeurs de Sauvages Ameriquains Comparees aux Moeurs de Premiers Temps* is an image that I continue to find hard to resist. It pricks and frees my imagination not only onto the nature of the administrator's action, but, more importantly in terms of the focus of this chapter, what kind of world in which such a move was taken and how such action was experienced.[2] The image shown in Figure 1.1 is fascinating in its representation of the type of syndrome and dynamics, disturbance and the violence and arrogance and hubris that Achebe points to in the spare words in his novel. Lafitau's image may be worth a thousand words; Achebe's spare words evoke a thousand more images. Lafitau's image does not so much fill in blanks left by Achebe as it makes Achebe's story a universal and more poignant telling about the conditions under which things began to fall apart, and what obtained before things fell apart. I am concerned in this chapter primarily with what light the image casts on the village world on which Achebe focuses.

I continue to profit from following Michel de Certeau's rather fascinating interpretation of the image.[3] With him I see in the image the racialized (white European) and gendered (female) inscriber of history and transcendent stable meaning and truth. The white woman in this case is seated in relationship to what looks to be Father Time and Death. She writes about the Truth as the world she represents orders it. This means writing in order to clarify, among other things, how the Others—savages and primitives, strange, wild, inferior—recently

Figure 1.1 Scotin, Gérard Jean-Baptiste (1671–1716) [Allegory with figures.]
1724. From: Lafitau, Joseph-François. *Moeurs des sauvages ameriquaines,
compares aux moeurs des premiers temps*—par le P. Lafitau; ouvrage enrichi
de figures en taille-douce. Museum national d'Histoire naturelle, Paris,
France. © RMN-Grand Palais/Art Resource, NY

"discovered," fit into the (new, early modern) scheme of things. Thus, we find them represented as objects, fetishes, trinkets, lying along the bottom of the image. The "truth" to be told and spun about these Others must involve a type of bricolage, assembling among the objects and placing them—and the collectives they represent—in some interpretive framework. Since these Others are not presumed to be able to speak, to communicate effectively, to know in the manner that counts—consider the "talking book" incident in Equiano's and many other slaves' narratives— they require no respectful gesture; they simply must be arranged in the new hierarchy and written up accordingly.

Although it may not be the kind of image or representation that directly inspired Achebe's storytelling, this image from the early eighteenth century is both a foretelling and a poignant reflection of the plight of the people of Achebe's story, of how their plight was wrought. Like the unnamed peoples of Lafitau's image, the people of Achebe's story were by an imperial power signified.[4]

The point to be made here in this chapter from Lafitau's striking frontispiece is that the characters in the story told by Achebe are emphatically *not* objects of the sort piled up and strewn on the floor of colonial violence. They *can* and *do* speak, they *can* and *do* feel, and so forth. And they speak and feel in realistic terms. They are interesting—funny, sad, tragic, strong, weak, pathetic, heroic, wise, silly, loving, narrow, over the top, vengeful, yearning, searching; they are human. They are in so many important respects universal. That they are depicted as such and that we as readers need not jump through mind-bending or second takes or great psychological leaps to see this is a tribute to the brilliance of Achebe's writing. It was not so before his work was published in the mid-twentieth century: black peoples had been in European literatures and in Western popular cultural representations generally heavily, unrelentingly, signified as flat, inert, silent, humiliated, effeminate, too noble, or sometimes too wily and wicked, an always too veiling yet colorful "darkness." Notwithstanding their differences in genre, Joseph Conrad's *Heart of Darkness* and the Hollywood-produced Tarzan movies are here conjured up.[5]

But then we are given in Achebe's *TFA* the gift of a story about these colorful and layered humans who, as it happens, have black skins and, as it also happens, are situated in the same tense period in which Conrad wrote, the turn of the nineteenth into the twentieth century. This is the time and situation when the turning, the falling apart of things, is advanced and is seen to be fateful, at a critical point. The humans in the story are arresting figures whose humanness, in spite of all that goes on, in spite of the violence done within their own ranks and to them, is the point of the story. There is in the novel no dark savage-filled jungle—urban or rural.[6] There is no natural savagery or unrelenting darkness or belatedness or ignorance that marks only these particular humans. On the contrary, what readers are provided in the novel is a fascinating open window onto parts of the all at once complexly stabilizing rhythms and traditions and weaknesses and foibles of a traditional village in an Igbo-inflected African setting into which a part of the outside world breaks with violence and its profound perduring consequences. Things may have been already fragile; the world that was the village in focus may have been already vulnerable, but the falling of the white men upon the village was also decisive in the falling apart.

It is an amazing picture—because modern readers had not really seen such before the publication of Chinua Achebe's *TFA*. This realistic, richly textured painted-by-a-person-of-the-Black-Atlantic picture, a picture of local traditional life among black peoples in an "African" setting—with focus not on the "Tarzan" character but on fully developed and complex local (black) humanity—was a shock to the system, to social and thinking habits and reading formations firmly controlled by the European colonial order of things, including the order of representations and media in the twentieth century. North Atlantic worlds had been socialized not to expect to see, not to think possible, the representation and reality of such a world—a world in which black peoples are not overdetermined by the twisted invention of "Africa." Before Achebe's *TFA* most of us—including "Africans"—were generally disposed to picture "Africa" as "dark Africa"—that is, through the eyes of varieties of "white men" who were themselves deeply invested and implicated in and imprisoned by the adventures and economics, the politics and structures, the ideologies, of the colonial world. *Pacification of the Primitive*, indeed.

For my purposes in this book, the thick and complex and rich representation of traditional village life, especially its central/centering rituals, sensibilities, and orientation, is important. The Umuofia village in *TFA* as representation of an orientation, a sensibility, an epistemic system, including a certain felt anxiety, is particularly important.

Several passages seemed designed to represent the color and texture, rhythms and movement, sounds and dynamics that make the local village life come alive and make the reader want to know and experience more. One of the earliest of such passages in the novel describes a call to a community gathering in response to an urgent and traumatic event—the "murder" of a "daughter of Umuofia." No typical, certainly no everyday event in terms of substance, perhaps. But I should like to draw attention to the call itself as form and to the realistic and typical ritual elements and functions that are recorded:

> In the morning the market-place was full. There must have been about ten thousand men there, all talking in low voices. At last Ogbuefi Ezeugo stood up in the midst of them and bellowed four times, "*Umuofia kwenu*," and on each occasion he faced a different direction and seemed to push the air with a clenched fist. And ten thousand men answered "*Yaa!*" each time.[7]

Here we have a glimpse of the community being *called*—literally *called together*. Without the modern technology that we have come to take for granted, the call was to those who are assumed to be pretty much within earshot. About this matter more to be discussed below, but for the moment it is important to make clear that this was indication of the limited extension, the finite reach of definition and physical boundaries, of the community. The community being described was traditional-local in self-understanding and orientation as well as in extension. Almost everyone was known; all were separated, if at all, by only a degree or two. One was understood to belong to the

32

community insofar as one was literally present in the community, the extent to which one's body was counted or could be accounted for, the extent to which one could hear the call. One's identity was where one was located. You were *where* you were. You were who you were because you were *here*, not there.

"*Umuofia kwenu*" ("*Umuofia*, listen") was the call to the clan, a "formulaic" greeting made by Ogbuefi Ezeugo. The latter was one among those who had attained the rank of *ozo*, one of the august titles of respected figures in the community. Only such a figure had the *auctoritas* to call the clan together (*TFA*, 8, n#3).

"*Umuofia*" is the name of the community being named, being called and called to attention. It was understood to be one of several precolonial Igbo villages in the land that is now located within the "independent" but unsurprisingly troubled and confounding nation-state that is on the other side of the formal colonial system called "Nigeria." Such villages were often complexly federated for the sake of ensuring some degree of protection against common enemies and challenges (*TFA*, 3, n#1). There were often tensions between neighboring villages. The name "*Umuofia*" that Achebe gives to the village at the center of the novel means "people of the forest." It was likely intended by Achebe to convey something of the rustic or traditional if not ideal circumstance of precolonial days (*TFA*, xiv–xxi). Certainly, the name registers the importance of place, a particular appropriate orientation to it, and identity and meaning in relationship to it. Identity and meaning and knowing—these we are clearly meant to reflect that knowing or consciousness turned around place, around orientation to it, around various types of positions and participation in it.

And there is the now-famous description of the ongoing gatherings—the communal ceremonies—of the clan. These gatherings were ostensibly and typically called to address some particular question or problem or matter—property disputes or domestic problems, rivalries, and the like—requiring the wise judgment of the elders, who were understood to represent the dead but nevertheless paradoxically always present ancestors. Descriptions of responses to the ritual dance performances would seem to suggest that more was usually at issue than trials and the adjudications of this or that dispute. Among the more things at issue were such matters as grounding, the reaffirmation of belonging, the re-presentation of the subtending communal myth that reminded all about who and what and where they were. Everyone understood that such ceremonies, which usually began "when the sun's heat had softened" (53), rendered lyrically through indirect or veiled means—as ritual play[8]—ultimately came from the "spirits of the ancestors," and were to be accepted as such by all. Such acceptance guaranteed belonging, identity construction, stasis, including a type of manipulation or management of meaning (and behavior).

The rituals and performances of the ceremonies enthralled all, notwithstanding the obvious male-centric focus and patriarchal privileges. The women were at such gatherings expected to sit or stand back, to observe "from the fringe like outsiders"(53).[9] There was clear evidence of the universal problem with—the fear of—difference. The latter, in this case in regard to gender, certainly, but there were throughout the story other stations and conditions, natural and otherwise, that were viewed as threatening because they were different from what had been constructed and learned and established as a certain stasis, arrangement, normalcy in all areas and domains. These differences in stations and conditions included appearance, language or speech, behavior, belief. These differences were understood to eat away at, tear, the naturalized fabric of community. They were noted and were understood out of a sense of security and fear to require collective and individual actions or responses. Dealing with differences prompted actions that ranged from (self-)isolation, persecution, pity, at times even to execution.[10]

Achebe's description of the backdrop and context for what we are to take as a typical ceremonial gathering—allowing the spare and quiet and sensitive voice of an ambivalent narrator who seems to be the outsider who nonetheless registers some sensitivity, attachment, and intimacy of relationship—is too rich and textured not to be quoted here:

> The titled men and elders sat on their stools waiting for the trials to
> begin. There were nine of them ...

34

An iron gong sounded, setting up a wave of expectation in the crowd. Everyone looked in the direction of the *egwugwu* house. *Gome, gome, gome* went the gong, and a powerful flute blew a high-pitched blast. Then came the voices of the *egwugwu*, guttural and awesome. The wave struck the women and children and there was a backward stampede. But it was momentary. They were already far enough where they stood and there was room for running away if any of the *egwugwu* should go towards them.

The drum sounded again and the flute blew.[11] The *egwugwu* house was now a pandemonium of quavering voices: *Aru oyim de de de dei!* filled the air as the spirits of the ancestors, just emerged from the earth, greeted them in their esoteric language ...

Aru oyim de de de dei! flew around the dark, closed hut like tongues of fire. The ancestral spirits of the clan were abroad. The metal gong beat continuously now and the flute, shrill and powerful, floated on the chaos.

And then the *egwugwu* appeared. The women and children sent up a great shout and took to their heels. It was instinctive. A woman fled as soon as the *egwugwu* came in sight. And when, as on that day, nine of the greatest masked spirits in the clan came out together it was a terrifying spectacle ...

Each of the nine *egwugwu* represented a village of the clan. Their leader was called Evil Forest. Smoke poured out of his head ...

"*Umuofia kwenu!*" [he] shouted ..., pushing the air with his raffia arms. The leaders of the clan replied, "*Yaa!*"

"*Umuofia kwenu!*"

"*Yaa!*"

"*Umuofia kwenu!*"

"*Yaa!*" (53–54)

Much drama, to be sure, led into and outward from this moment in the short but intense novel. But in this passage we are provided in nuce— parts of which are repeated elsewhere—the terms around which, the conditions in which, all persons in that world belonged, were shaped, identified, came to be known, and came into consciousness and came to know. Who they are and how the world is ordered are made clear in the passage, or, more correctly, in the ritual play—only a partial description of which is included. Perhaps the *partial* description of the ritual in the novel helps make the point about its significance: Who, after all, could know and tell all the mysteries involved? The narrator could only point to the ritual, not exegete it, not contain it. The fathoming and excavation and unfolding of the meaning of the ritual seem to be the point of the novel itself.

Everything in the novel in some respects seems to relate to or revolve around the ritual as described. In it the community is named—and is literally and dramatically called out—"*Umuofia kwenu*"—for recognition and for gathering around various issues and for various purposes. In relationship to it, groups of persons and individuals are given identity, differentiated, and placed in positions of relative hierarchy. The major character Okonkwo rises and falls and rises and falls throughout the story and meets his ultimate fate precisely in relationship to what the ritual signifies. The agricultural yield in yams[12] is measured and acknowledged and celebrated or bemoaned on such occasions. In sum, the ritual represents a centering reality—that reality by which one knows the self and the truth about the world. The ritual does not merely represent or contain or convey meaning—as in some substantive point or message; it does not so much lead to meaning; it is itself meaning *per-formed*.[13] It performs the meaning that is too much or too deep to be brought into language by any one person. It can only be experienced in the context of the dance on the part of those spirits—the ancestors—who are represented by the masked ones, the elders within the village.

In the ritual the elders *mask* meaning: they do not in simple terms veil or hide meaning; this is not so much, I should like to argue, about secrecy as about managing (or, as in all turns or stages to be discussed in this book, attempting to manage) meaning. Drawing on an expansive representation of human forms of communication—sights, sounds, symbolic movements, gestures—they dramatize the community's ways of thinking, ways or terms of knowing itself and the world. They reveal something precisely through the apparent "veiling," understood less as holding back something than communicating complexly—in other words, "hitting a lick with a crooked stick,"[14] through indirection.

So it seems that individuals in this community know—themselves, others, the larger world—through the carapace, the filter, the (dancing) masks, which eerily, hauntingly usher them into the presence of the ancestor spirits, somewhat playfully (but not unseriously), furtively, and complexly represented by the leading males of the clan, the *egwugwu*. Through their ritual performances, the *egwugwu* essentially perform for the members of the whole community—re-present to them—who they are. And, again, who they are is dictated by where they are. The ancestors, it is assumed, could not be found and addressed and worshipped and venerated anywhere; they are only *there*—in that place, in that village. None of the actions or pronouncements would make sense outside of that place.

So what sort of world is this? How is it constituted? Not so much in terms of this or that figurehead, this or that family or dynasty, but in terms of a logic of formation? In other words, how does it cohere? How does it mean? And how is meaning made within it? How does one come to know—self and others and world—within it? How is knowledge transmitted or communicated? How is it authorized, naturalized, and made compelling? And what does the ritual and responses to it and to the world around it reveal about what Okonkwo as main character, especially, fears, becomes anxious about?

These are questions that *TFA* both provokes and provides glimpses into. Although the novel can be pressed into many different types of conversations with their interests and agenda, I should like here to use it—particularly the window onto the texture and rhythms of village life—to think with mainly about how humans came to organize themselves, how they have projected their thinking and feelings, their hopes and fears, their aspirations and anxieties. And how and why they have constructed knowledge and managed that knowledge, made it natural and authoritative. *TFA* casts light on this dynamic in a rather provocative manner—by this I mean the novelistic form. This form[15] affords the possibility not merely of a more realistic picture of the matters and issues that are pertinent, but of the needed provocation toward

37

an expansion of the range and type of questions and issues pertaining to the topic and its dynamics. Even more important, it includes what I discern to be at the very least traces or outlines of the three major turns in the dialectics—what I call *scriptura-lectics*—of human knowledge construction and management.

My use of Achebe's *TFA* in this chapter entails tracing the outline of a realistic picture of a local traditional village life (that happens to be situated in west Africa) as an example of a type of social formation with its own system of meaning, knowledge, communication, and conscientization, not inert trinkets strewn along Europe's floor. This system I understand as an iteration of a significant early development in, scripturalectics. This first stage in scripturalectics I call, following the language in the story Achebe has woven—*mask-ing*; in ultimate terms and at the most basic level, the stage is a response to, and reflection of, gendered fear and anxiety. Although not often referenced in discussions about the functions of the mask in historical cultures, I maintain that the mask is quite important as site and sign—as that object on which and sign with which is constructed and construed knowledge, or, rather, the *management* of (claims about) knowledge as the *management* of (male-specific) fear.

A bigger canvas—not so much the largest and finalized one—onto which a broader perspective and compelling theorizing argument may be thrown is in order. I should like to do this by discussing briefly (1) the period in the stage of evolutionary development of human consciousness and sociality in which the dynamics depicted in *TFA* may fall; (2) the functions of ritual within such a period of evolutionary development; and (3) the role of the mask/masquerade in comparative and historical-evolutionary social relations and dynamics.

Drawing first on the late well-known sociologist Robert N. Bellah and on what ended up being his last and most accomplished work— *Religion in Human Evolution: From the Paleolithic to the Axial Age* (2011), arguably the most recent and most expansive critical theorizing treatment of the subject of human evolution—I place the world of *TFA* in the category of "tribal" religion or culture. For Bellah this category was a descriptor of small-scale societies that included hunter-gatherers as well as horticulturalists and pastoralists. It included forms of consciousness and the "production of meaning"[16] in a form of sociality and organization that was mostly local, not radically extensive, and less complexly stratified if not organized than what would later develop into "early states or early civilizations," or "archaic" societies (e.g., ancient Mesopotamia Egypt; Shang and Western Zhou China).

But care needs to be taken to understand that this evolutionary stage called "tribal" did not somehow appear in some distant past and disappear before the onset of more layered and complex societies; the tribal societies in fact perdure in some important respects and in admittedly unusual and remote situations even in the modern era, as Bellah's examples of the Navajo and the Walbiri (Australian Aborigines) and the Kalapalo (central Brazil) make clear.[17] In almost all the respects that he argued about such societies, the category "tribal" is an apt description of the late-nineteenth-century Umuofia—a placeholder for a world Achebe knows and partly pines and mourns for, partly criticizes and translates for the reader in *TFA*.

Bellah sees in tribal societies several characteristics, the most important of which he understood to be the central importance of *ritual*. The latter is seen as a prime example of and site for the demonstration of symbolization and uses of language. The term "musilanguage" is used by Bellah to capture ritual as this language—the combination of types of communication and play, communication as play.[18] The latter is not the opposite of seriousness or work; it involves complex gestures and types of contact and communication. And it becomes the most important means by which tribal societies—as baseline, of a sort, for all societies overlapping with and succeeding them—are ordered. Ritual facilitates "the production of meaning" and all that pertains to it, including, I would add, its management or control. Ritual is "society enacting itself ... [it is] constitutive of the very society it makes possible."[19]

Bellah's more important and pointed, if not original, argument about ritual has to do with functionality. Ritual, he asserts, must not be thought of as merely mirroring reality; on the contrary, "It gives a picture of reality as it *ought* to be."[20] It also binds society: It pulls all the basic aspects or elements together in unity. Consider, for example, those rituals or parts of rituals in which chaos or disorder is performed or depicted again and again *as if* being transcended, overwhelmed. Such performance serves to bind performers and observers in solidarity in and over against the chaos. The latter has been experienced in terms of simply not knowing—why or when or how things happen or are as they are. To experience chaos is not to know, to be without meaning.

The earliest specialists or virtuosi in ritual are imaged—notwithstanding their being called by different names across cultures and times—as priests, magicians, therapists/healers of some sort. Rituals of healing have always been and continue to be the best-known or most important of the rituals.[21] This suggests that ritual may have developed as it did in association with the understandably pressing concern or anxiety about the mystery of sickness and death. There is something quite poignant about societies that in so many different ways name or acknowledge and respect such persistent fears.

Bellah does not much elaborate—except to draw on historian of religion Jonathan Z. Smith in making the point that one of the chief functions of ritual is to achieve "*a controlled environment*" in a situation in which otherwise "the variables ... of ordinary life may be displaced *precisely* because they are felt to be so overwhelmingly present and powerful." Ritual, then, comes to be understood as "a means of performing the way things ought to be in conscious tension to the way things are in such a way that this ... ritualized [!] perfection is recollected in the ordinary, uncontrolled, course of things."[22]

How does ritual actually accomplish the control needed and sought? Through a kind of language use. With the redundancy, generated by the expectancy of the tempo, and the rhythms created by drums, hand- or feet-clapping, and so forth, ritual transforms what otherwise might be considered meaningless noises into "highly condensed ... referentially-emotively meaningful, sound events." As a kind of "musilanguage," ritual thereby means.[23]

It is at this point in his argument that Bellah turned to the scholar whose book, *Ritual and Meaning in the Making of Humanity* (1999), he considered "the most serious effort" on ritual up to that time—the late anthropologist Roy Rappaport.[24] Bellah turns to Rappaport to gain support for his argument that ritual heals and binds and provides clarity in an existence in which *"things keep coming apart."*[25] Sidestepping the persistent argument in some circles about whether ritual precedes myth, Bellah draws on Rappaport's rather straightforward definition of ritual—"the performance of more or less invariant sequences of formal acts and utterances not entirely encoded by the performers"[26]—in order to advance his argument that ritual is "remarkably stable," is more resistant to change than myth, and, with *invariance* as its central feature, facilitates human capacity for symbol-making.[27]

It is worth my noting here that Rappaport also argued that ritual was not simply "symbolic representation of the social contract," not merely another way of saying something, but instead is "the social act basic to humanity."[28] Those engaging in ritual, according to Rappaport, constituted a "congregation."[29] Within the latter, rituals are seen to carry or perform a special, proto-"language"—"words" through which any thing can be conceived. From the proliferation and performances of multiple "words," "the Word" is conceived: "the very invariance of canon is a meta-message concerning the word it includes; these words and not others."[30] Rituals take on meaning not so much from each of the different parts—*significata*, words—but from the "union" of such.[31] They are seen to "unite ... the psychic, social, natural or cosmic processes,"[32] to "mend ... worlds forever breaking apart under the blows of daily usage and the slashing distinction of language."[33] As their "metaperformativeness" comes to be seen as unquestionable, beyond reproach, naturalized, rituals are seen to reflect "times out of times,"[34] and a type of sanctification is ascribed to them. It is in fact the sanctification of rituals that establishes the language that then becomes "the Word"—the "sacred Word" that reflects and submits to ritual's invariance.[35]

That this situation leads to a circular structure of authority—the "cybernetics of the holy"[36]—which, with the cultivation of writing can be, indeed has all too often become, vicious—what we often today recognize and refer to with that freighted term "fundamentalism"—can be easily enough discerned, if not easily understood, addressed, and resisted.[37] Before the onset and development of writing cultures the "*apparent* invariance," or the "*claim* to invariance" was simply that: a claim, a fiction that was honored, an agreed-on suspension. With writing, the suspension was over time set aside;[38] the "apparent" became that which perdured, that which became essential, eternal, natural.

We are here provided a snapshot of and perspective on how ritual developed and changed, but what remains to be elaborated on is the motor for it. The speculative notion that it was motored by a felt crisis, fear and anxiety over something, perhaps, having to do with sickness and death, was not elaborated on by Bellah. It is easy enough—even if we do not want to focus on it, but want instead always to deny it, run away from it—to concede that fear and anxiety over such matters are always at issue. The real puzzle is about how the fear is manifested, how the fear is projected, whether and on what terms it is denied or explained away or otherwise engaged—or managed. I am very much concerned in this book about precisely these matters: I should like to explore, using the concepts and phenomena of scriptures/scripturalizing/scripturalization, what sorts of fear and anxiety haunt us and what work we make them—the fear and the scriptures—do for and to us.

Having argued that it is a (type of) masquerade ritual or ritual as masquerade that is central to Achebe's story about who the Umuofians were—before things fell apart—and having engaged Bellah in order to facilitate wider thinking about ritual as part of the evolution of social formation and formation of consciousness, I should like now to draw attention to the work and issue-raising of a few other theorists who have taken up the matter of the function of ritual as part of a schema of the evolutionary stages of human consciousness. Among the several issues that are broached or addressed by these theorists—either in direct or indirect terms, sometimes only implied, but always provoking more and stronger implications and arguments and questions— are those having to do with the motoring, facilitating, reflecting and refracting fears and anxieties. After wedging the arguments of these theorists into the discussion, I shall return to Bellah and finally to Achebe with concluding words for the concerns of this chapter.

I should like to turn first to the scholar on whom Bellah draws most, at least in his argument about evolutionary stages: the psychologist Merlin Donald. In his fascinating book *A Mind So Rare: The Evolution of Human Consciousness* (2001), Donald provides a schematic of the transitions or stages in the evolution of human cognition and culture toward the emergence of "a symbolizing mentality" (260).[39] This evolution is, according to Donald, really tension between "culture" and the continuous expansion of "conscious capacity." There are four stages in his schema: episodic, mimetic, mythic, and theoretic.[40]

The very first stage in consciousness and cognition—the episodic—is by Donald actually bracketed and unnumbered. That is because he considers it to be the baseline: It represents the world of primates and involves awareness of the self and of others in reactions to certain stimuli, events, or episodes. But what inspires the schema and serves as focus of the most detailed attention are the transitions in consciousness that emerge from this baseline.

So the first *numbered* stage of transition—the mimetic—occurred when the stone tool–using, meat-eating, culture-cultivating, if not language-using, hominid species first appeared. This was more than two million years ago. It was the cognitive capacity that was the mimetic skill that was new and significant. This skill involved "playacting, body language, precise imitation, and gesture." Not yet language that we might recognize, but expressivity, sounds, voice manipulations—all in the service of communicating and solidifying group mentality.

The second transition stage—the mythic—began with the appearance of "archaic *Homo sapiens*," approximately half a million years ago, progressing to our species *Homo sapiens sapiens*, appearing approximately 125,000 years ago. With this transition more sophisticated tools and other objects were invented and used; migrations over vast areas of the planet are in evidence; and spoken language was cultivated to the point of producing rich oral cultures, the baseline of human culture up to the present.

The third stage—the theoretic—began approximately 40,000 years ago. It is characterized by a revolution in the technology of symbols, symbolization, and externalization of memory. The invention of "external symbolic devices" to store and retrieve cultural knowledge was and remains revolutionary. Such devices facilitate our knowledge of previous stages in cognition and consciousness and thereby thicken it, increase its potential for reflexive thinking.

Donald offers for each transition stage an argument or speculation about what tripped humans onto the next stage. The arguments mainly have to do with invention and uses of tools, but I note a curious inclusion on the table he provided (Figure 1.2) that comprises columns labeled Stage (Episodic, Mimetic, Mythic, Theoretic), Species/Period, Novel Forms, Manifest Change, and the question-begging heading Governance. We find as categories under Governance "episodic and reactive," "mimetic styles and archetypes," "mythic framework," and "institutionalized paradigmatic thought and invention" crossed with the four stages of cognition and consciousness. With the categories of Governance placed so in his theoretical schema, I wonder whether

TABLE 7.1

Successive layers in the evolution of human cognition and culture. Each stage continues to occupy its cultural niche today, so that fully modern societies have all four stages simultaneously present.

Stage	Species/Period	Novel Forms	Manifest Change	Governance
EPISODIC	Primate	Episodic event perceptions	Self-awareness and event sensitivity	Episodic and reactive
MIMETIC (first transition)	Early hominids, peaking in *H. erectus* 2M-0.4 Mya	Action metaphor	Skill, gesture, mime, and imitation	Mimetic styles and archetypes
MYTHIC (second transition)	Sapient humans, peaking in *H. sapiens sapiens* 0.5 Mya-present	Language, symbolic representation	Oral traditions, mimetic ritual, narrative thought	Mythic framework of governance
THEORETIC (third transition)	Modern culture	External symbolic universe	Formalisms, large-scale theoretic artifacts, massive external storage	Institutionalized paradigmatic thought and invention

Figure 1.2 "Table 7.1," from *A Mind So Rare: The Evolution of Human Consciousness* by Merlin Donald. Copyright © 2001 by Merlin Donald. Used by permission of W.W. Norton & Company, Inc.

Donald intended (or could be made here) to speak to the issue of influences and determinants, power and control? Fear and anxiety? These subjects do not seem to me ever to be far from a psychologist's interest, if not purview.

There is no extended discussion of such issues by Donald except at the very end of his book, in the last section of the chapter entitled "The Triumph of Consciousness" and in the Coda. In these sections Donald suggests that the "ultimate triumph of consciousness" may be associated with the cultivation of external symbols to the point of making culture the manufacturer of "virtual realities." Such symbols, as the work of culture, have profound impact on us, on our self-reflexive thinking, "making experience the object of its own deliberate capacities to plan."[41] Of course, there is recognition that the same arrangements can deceive, confuse, obfuscate. This can lead to the human mind being played, programmed, *script(uraliz)ed*.

It is important, therefore, to recognize how things work—that is, how cognition and consciousness are arranged in stages and how they are interrelated. Another helpful way of understanding how this works, how we are made conscious, is to image the situation in terms of representations (Figure 1.3). Corresponding to the stages of cognition and consciousness are what Donald calls the "evolved layers of human mind and cognition," "concentric rings": In the center ring are, as might be expected, episodes, as "a stream of discrete events" as "natural units of experience"; with mimetic representations are attitudes, gestures, postures, and so forth, setting forth the basic rules for all communication and expression; linguistic representations, in which are encoded and communicated with precision and efficiency stories,

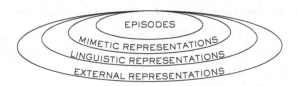

Figure 1.3 "Figure 8.4," from *A Mind So Rare: The Evolution of Human Consciousness* by Merlin Donald. Copyright © 2001 by Merlin Donald. Used by permission of W.W. Norton & Company, Inc.

myths, traditions; and finally, the even more precise system of collection and communication in external representations.[42]

How these circles are related and what seems to be at stake in the reality that they point to is what Donald tries to articulate—even if not as clearly as I would like. He addresses the matter somewhat obliquely, by invoking terms such as "control," "govern," "dominating," as he argues that the circles of representations are a unit—with the outer layers based on the inner layers—and that power and control lie in awareness of the power and control in the collective—in "culture":

> The unity of this sprawling cognitive-cultural system ... can be seen in the flow control through the three evolved layers of human mind and culture. The core episodic layer ... is inherently other-directed. It observes the world from an unselfconscious perspective. In contrast, the mimetic layer is acutely self-conscious ... The mimetic imagination is a dramatic actor. It gives culture shape, by using essentially the same set of conscious operations as an episodic mind, in a wider theater of action.
>
> The narrative layer adds greatly to this ... system. It gives ideas a certain autonomy from personal experience and creates the possibility of abstract beliefs and public discourse. But narrative constructions can govern the larger cognitive-cultural system only if they are successful in dominating the mimetic layer ... Narrative imagination wins control by altering the mimetic templates of culture and bringing them in line with myth. The chain of command is clear: Words and stories will dominate only if they successfully influence role paying, skill, and style. Myth gains power only when it directly controls the mimetic imagination. Mythmaking has become an important industry in our cultural hierarchy, and it usually emerges victorious. But its victories never destroy the unity of conscious experience because ... language floats on the surface of a very deep cognitive ocean. It has no autonomy. It cannot shatter the basic unity of experience and imagination because like episodic and mimetic cognition, it is rooted there.[43]

I understand Donald to argue here that these stages and transitions in collective cognition represent stages in increasing efficiency of control and exercise of power. What the reach for more efficient power and control is motored by remains to be fathomed.

Felicitas D. Goodman was by training and trade a linguist and anthropologist. She was perhaps best known for her field research work on altered states of consciousness. *Ecstasy, Ritual, and Alternate Reality: Religion a Pluralistic World* (1988)[44] I find to be a fascinating example of her thinking about human consciousness and other several other topics, including human evolution, the origins and evolution of religious behavior. The book first (Part One) makes the theoretical argument about how best to analyze human evolution. Such analysis should cross the independent variable of human life (interaction with the habitat) with dependent variables (the various second-order, social-culturalist responses). Part Two (Ethnography) of her book represents the actual elaborate analysis of the evolved human; it isolates five types of human sociality and analyzes each with respect to the several dependent variables that had been named. Although it seems clear that Goodman's longstanding main interest was in accounting for alternate reality and ecstatic behaviors, we have in her tightly drawn and crisply written analysis the crossing of the five types of human sociality (ethnography) with the various social-culturalist arrangements (dependent variables), contributing to a major analytical-interpretive schema of the evolution of the human. Hunter-gatherers, horticulturalists, agriculturalists, nomadic pastoralists, and city dwellers are discussed in terms of ritual behavior, the religious trance, alternate reality, fortunes and the rituals of divination, ethics, and the "semantics" of "religion."

There should be little surprise that ritual plays an important role among "dependent variables"—in terms of culture and culture-making. All other variables listed by Goodman revolve around or devolve from ritual. It is ritual and the refractions of ritual that seem to be the focus of human activity and orientation. Ultimately, what appears to be at stake is the capacity for experiencing that alternate reality in which "power hovers." In such reality—induced by the usual practices of ritual (sounds, tempo, movements)—one is invested with "new abilities ... award[ed] protection ... blessings and good fortune." One is also able to see things differently, and this seeing of things differently is also reflected (differently) in cultural types (ethnography). So

> the hunter-gatherers meet the spirit counterparts or aspects of the animals of ordinary reality, and upon death, they hunt and love just as they did when still alive. The horticulturalists see villages identical to their earthly ones. For desert nomads, the home of the spirits of the dead is lush and green. The tillers who were good kneel in adoration before their rulers, while the evil ones are forever banished to their various hells ... the urbanites are united with a few relatives and friends in a realm of light.[45]

But those in such a state had best beware: Alternate reality may also sometimes be the source of "misfortune," in which case divination—ironically, more and different kinds of religious ritual or religious protections of some kind—may be needed.[46]

The larger argument made by Goodman turns around the notion that each stage in evolution represents a stage in alienation from habit, with the corresponding increase in anxiety and fear and violence and chaos. Rituals not only name the problem, they also help address it: They provide ways to "cure" the sick or "save" the lost or assuage the guilt brought on by the strained or violent relationship with the habitat ("Mother Earth").[47] Precisely how these ways prove to be effective is not made clear.

Pierre Lévy defines himself as a scholar of cyberculture and social communication. His books *Collective Intelligence: Mankind's Emerging World in Cyberspace* (1997)[48] and *Cyberculture* (2001)[49] have proved in many respects to be profoundly prophetic about and deeply analytical about historical and ongoing trends in social media and communications at the end of one century and the turn into another. I am most interested in Lévy's historical-interpretive-evolutionist analysis of human consciousness that frames his arguments about cyberintelligence and other matters. Especially in *Collective Intelligence*, Lévy provides several different interpretive schemas and paradigms in attempts to explain how humankind has historically come to know—itself and all things enveloping it. In bringing to bear in his argumentation anthropological categories, identity formation theoretics, semiotics, social and cultural history, and epistemology, Lévy provides a basic but complex evolutionary schema of collective human knowing in terms of what he calls four anthropological/epistemological "spaces": the Earth, Territory, Commodity, and Knowledge. The emphasis on the spatial is important: It suggests even more strongly the importance of place and orientation in terms of construction and construal of knowledge systems.[50]

So with the Earth as baseline "world of signification," it is the (first) space that is "always already there," "the cosmos in which humanity communicates with animals, plans, landscapes, locales, and spirits." Corresponding to the Paleolithic period (spilling over into the Neolithic), it is that space that provides the baseline for what developed into human language and communication. It is in this space in which humankind lives harmoniously with everything around it, in a "process of unending re-creation." Humans hunted and foraged as they had need here and over there. Rituals are in this space construed to project and reflect back this sense of interrelatedness.[51]

The second space is the Territory. In this space with its new moment—Neolithic, 12,000 years ago, perhaps, up to the Second World War—a new reality that was the sedentary life, a sense of permanence developed, with all that this meant for the construction of culture and civilization. Agriculture, the village and the city, and writing developed. Territory was then seen needing to be divided, claimed, argued over and fought for, *described, measured,* and *inscribed.* Armies, scribes, tax collectors, religious organizations with their cathedrals and spires—these were required to safeguard or defend territory claimed and staked out. What soon (inevitably?) set in was a destructive, predatory view, an adversarial, dominating relationship with habitat. But the latter sometimes fights back. Chaos ensues: "rivers overflow their beds, the forest continues to grow, looters from the desert sack the hoard of treasure, women and men leave their fields and homes behind."[52] In this situation there has developed increased power and control for some few individuals over the many others, at times apart from, but more often in relationship to, the state or king or nation or church or some other larger collectives or regimes requiring the domination of others.

The third space is Commodity. With modifications along the way, to be sure, it is the "space," according to Lévy, in which "we" have lived since the eighteenth century. Capitalism as commodity space is inherently, fundamentally deterritorializing. It is so through circulation and manipulation of capital. It thereby represents a new order:

> Crossing borders, upsetting territorial hierarchies, the dance of money brought in its wake an accelerated movement, a rising tide of objects, signs, and individuals. Steamboats, railroads, automobiles, roads, accidents, highways, junkyards, trucks, cargo, tankers, airplanes, subways, transport, market outlets, circulation, distribution, saturation, motionless speed.[53]

The territorial space is not destroyed by the commodity space; the former subordinates the latter, organizes and uses it for its interests. Territory is "distended, hybridized, crisscrossed, cracked, disjointed, enveloped."[54]

The Fourth space is Knowledge. A space so called is not supposed to exist anywhere in particular, not in literal terms. It is at once a *u*-topia—no place—and not an earthly "paradise." The relationship between the other spaces and this one is complex: The collective intelligence that is the Knowledge space aims not to destroy the Earth, Territory, or Commodity; the perdurance of the three spaces is "conditioned" by the "new plane of existence for humanity" that the Knowledge space represents.[55]

I find the interpretive schemas of human evolutionary consciousness of Donald, Goodman, and Lévy, albeit different in many important respects, to be not only provocative and illuminating but somewhat similar in other important respects. They all are in conversation with Bellah's challenge to us to take note of the place of ritual in human evolution. Ritual seems not merely to be a part of one stage or period in evolution, but an ongoing basic and fundamental feature of humanness—of human cognition, discourse, projection, structuring of reality, as well as the complex and powerful register and translator of human fears and anxieties.

Inspired first by Achebe's story of the ritual play among the Umuofians and challenged by Bellah and other theorists of human evolution with whom we have been in conversation about the place and functions of rituals, it is worth an effort to fathom more deeply and specifically the matter of the work we make ritual do for us as humans. By "work" here I now mean specifically to try to get a handle on the nature of the fear and anxiety that affect and inspire, determine and motor sensibilities and orientation. Having been reminded by Achebe's realistic fiction about how humans come together, I propose to do this by allowing if not the richer, certainly the more richly displayed and registered, texture of ritual in another traditional village to be used to think with and compare to Umuofia.

I turn to another scholar of ritual, but one on whom Bellah did not draw: structuralist anthropologist Richard P. Werbner. Werbner's *Ritual Passage, Sacred Journey: The Process and Organization of Religious Movement* (1989)[56] is a vigorous and interesting reengagement of structuralist thinking. He argues that the latter is worth reconsideration and reapplication as he draws on historical analysis—with acute sensitivity to colonial, neocolonial, and nationalist interests—and field research in advancing the concept of ritual as passage. With focus on cults and other formations in southern and western Africa and New Guinea, he argues for ritual passage as a fruitful and sharp analytical wedge for a wide range of social dynamics, relations, and phenomena. His work is divided into two major parts: ritual passage and sacred journey. These parts were designed to cast light on both the types and aspects of rituals performed (Part I) and the types of organizations and formations that are produced from or in association with such rituals (Part II).

It is in his Chapter 4, "Umeda Masquerade: Renewing Identity and Power in the Cosmos," that Werbner provides the fullest critical theoretical and ethnographically based and informed discussion about the ritual that is the masquerade. With focus on the *ida* festival in the village of Umeda in the New Guinea lowlands, Werbner takes the reader on a fascinating journey into the dynamics within a village located in but nonetheless oriented far outside the modern world. It thereby opens a window onto the world Achebe describes for his reader, a world positioned on the margins of the modern world, forced into grappling with it from a position of dislocation and humiliation. Werbner's interest in fathoming what the masking ritual in the world of Umeda was all about, in shedding some light on the work it was made to do, very much reflects and captures my interest. I turn to him (and related discussions) as a means of summarizing and making pointed my argument about what is at stake in this first stage of scripturalectics.

Werbner pays due deference to those who have made provocative arguments about ritual in general and have done extensive fieldwork in and on Umeda in particular,[57] but he does not shrink from making an aggressive and pointed argument about the function of the masquerade in Umeda and beyond and what this means for generalizing theorizing about the evolution of social consciousness. Masking induces and facilitates the psychic journeying or transport that he argues is basic to the ritual process that is in turn basic to psychosocial evolution and orientation. The mask as part of the ritualized festival is used to help articulate the joking (*mokus*) and the play (*modes*)[58]—the self-veiling or tricking of the self—necessary to help communities come to terms with reality as "an unstable unity of opposites."[59] What coming to terms effectively means is to be transformed, to go through a *rite de passage* à la van Gennep et al., to experience a metamorphosis of the sort referenced by Goodman (above). Such experience, what Werbner calls the "sacred journey," is called for in order to address complex and perduring issues and problems, "opposites" or, better, contradictions and paradoxes having to do with, for example (all from the male perspective, of course), outsiders who are potential enemies, or the ongoing relations with and duties in regard to women and family, sexual potency, and death.[60] The latter represent by far the most challenging problems. Werbner argues what is at stake by focusing on a set of "coordinate axes" that structure "opposing principles of exchange" that are part of a "vision of the giving and receiving of life and death."[61] Each activity engaged within the structure represents a type of boundary-crossing experience.

In his summarizing of the boundary-crossing or structure of exchange among the Umeda, Werbner is eloquent in his statement of the general problem and the proposed resolution and thereby provides a wider perspective on what may be considered the primary motor for the general phenomenon of ritual masking:

> the Principle of Giving implies the Principle of Receiving—neither can exist alone, or without the other. What is perhaps no so obvious is that such co-implication is paradoxical. It poses a dilemma for the [Umeda] villager when they annually renew their cosmos in masquerade. Human fertility threatens the abundance of game, and the more children a man fathers, the less he is expected to hunt or to be able to hunt. Similarly, killing vitiates commensality and, in the form of sorcery, becomes its ultimate perversion. In a festival for the best in eating, what place is there for killing? And in dancing, which is sexual expression, admittedly disguised in many ways, how is hunting to be given its due? In other words, the problem for the villagers is this: How are they to master the antitheses? All are essential, if the cosmos is to be renewed as a complete whole ... The difficulty is not to be resolved by striking a balance. Rather, it is a matter of renewing the cosmos as an order containing its own imbalances, its priorities, its hierarchy of values ... the villagers resolve the dilemma primarily by recourse to *humor and clowning* [my emphasis] and by requiring spectators to take matters into their own hands ... The resolution fits a dialectical vision that sees that the cosmos is ceaselessly destroying itself and being reborn only to die.[62]

It is the masking that is most closely associated with the clowning and taken most seriously by Werbner.[63] It is through ritual clowns and their clowning that the Umeda villagers "make sense" of the antitheses, the paradoxes—more precisely, the fears and anxieties—and in my view attempt to "manage" them. This management is achieved through putting everyday life in suspension—in the manner that Victor Turner understood the liminal phase of ritual passage[64]—and in bringing along women and children with the arrangement, the play. The masquerade facilitates the clowning that leads to the suspension in consciousness that results in the sacred journeying that is transformation:

> The performance of rebirth recreates masculine fantasies about the fundamentals of human order. In the masquerade, playing upon masculine androgyny, kinship is recast in a primordial form—the kinship of mothers, of daughters, of fathers, of sons. Enacted first, in a male form, are the relationships which, as daughters and mothers, women mediate over the *receiving* and the *giving* of life. Then come the relationships that, as fathers, men mediate over the *receiving* of death and, as sons, over *giving* it. The movement of the masquerade, given its core metaphor of male reproductive sexuality, follows a masculinized order of kinship ... what is *made known* [my emphasis] by and to the masqueraders is not merely something static: i.e. the way that relationships mirror each other. Rather, it is something dynamic. Each relationship is seen and felt, through ordeals and contradictions, to lead to its alternative ... The male masquerade is an unfolding of primordiality, of masculine androgyny. It is *as if* [my emphasis] men mask themselves in immortality only to recover their own mortality.[65]

In addition to Werbner's emphases (the giving and receiving in regard to dynamics of relationships), I should like to point out the importance of knowing—that is, what is revealed, "made known"—as that which is also very much at stake. What must come out of the metamorphosis facilitated by the masquerade festival is a certain type of awareness, knowing. This knowing is about how one is positioned within the world as it is ordered and reordered and as it falls into chaos. So the import of the masking is to facilitate the head-switching, the transformation, the sense of the "as if"[66] that is the basis of a knowing that is both in and beyond the regular order of things.

But the argument and discussion regarding the function of mask-ing I find most compelling—because it is wide-ranging and layered, historically informed, analytical, and comparative in orientation—is that by art historian and anthropologist A. Davie Napier in his book *Masks, Transformation, and Paradox* (1986).[67] Although primarily focused on preclassical Greece, Napier's book ranges over and con-structs arguments in relation to and draws conclusions from and about traditions that include Indo-European, Balinese, Indian, and Hindu, and beyond. His arguments also seem to have implications for the ongoing mixed-disciplinary analysis of the human. Although certainly not the first scholar to make the point about ambiguity, anxiety, fear, and insecurities in cultures as inspiration and provocation for mask-ing traditions, Napier uses masks to think with and argue strongly about change/difference/transformation as the fundamental and ongo-ing problem—paradox—in human social life. In his view, masks both reveal and cover up this problem, especially as it is exacerbated by instability or ambiguity of knowledge and perception, what he terms "the metaphysics of ambivalence."[68]

Napier seems most adept in naming this cross-cultural, arguably universal, problem and challenge in terms that are provocative and force engagement. For example, his discussion of the cross-cultural function of the mask is made to be a discussion about the challenge all humans have in coming to terms with apprehension, perception, illu-sion, complexity. We go to the mask, he argues, in order to acknowl-edge and represent complexity, change that we cannot account for. This is otherwise called the paradoxical—"the acceptance of what empiri-cally is not."[69] It leads to cultivation of the skills of "make-believe" and of what in science is termed hypothesizing. Because it is the human face that is the means of perceiving, the mask as disguise has become the primary means through which illusion and all that pertains to it may be worked, explored. In sum: "Masks are hypothetical and make-believe. They are paradoxical."[70]

Perhaps Napier's most important contribution to the discussion about masks has to do with his focus on them as part of the manipula-tion of the situation involving changing appearances or perceptions.

"Manipulation" may at first seem too strong, but it is an appropriately tensive term to capture the wide range of dynamics—from the social and political challenges brought on by difference to antinomies and the related and ensuing epistemological and interpretational problems.[71] Insofar as it represents transition, the mask also helps mediate or manipulate responses to the paradoxes inherent in transition. It turns us away from thinking ourselves secure in the "empirical account" and *provides an avenue for selective personification in manipulating certain recognized paradoxes.*[72] Of course, it comes as no surprise to Napier or to the rest of us that the most important of the paradoxes we have always had to face has to do with "creation, and destruction, birth and death." When we pay attention, masks help us teach ourselves that change—transition, transformation, the gap or jump in nature evolutionists call "saltation"—is a "precondition," not an "aberration," of the human and of existence in general.[73]

Drawing on the works of scholars of ancient Greece such as J. H. Croon and F. Altheim, Napier makes the case for the role of masks in Greek funerary rites, shamanistic practices, and exorcisms and within such contexts as a type of "manager" of conflicting and "illusionary" perceptions. Napier makes use of Croon's use of the now widely recognized episode of what is presumed to be gladiatorial games played out in the larger context of a funerary rite rendered on an Etruscan tomb-fresco at Tarquinia (Figure 1.4).[74]

The episode depicts a masked figure escorting another who appears to be a condemned man: The latter appears to be held tight by the rope controlled by the masked figure, has his head covered by a sack, and is attacked by the masked figure's dog. What is pointed out as being most important is the inscription of a word, *phersu* (Etruscan; it roughly translates into our English "person"), that appears to the left of the masked figure. Napier, following Croon who follows Altheim, understands the inscribed word to refer to the masked figure, not to the mask alone.

This point suggests that the function of the mask is to facilitate the management of the funereal performances—that is, the different perceptions and understandings of what takes place in the ritual. In

Figure 1.4 Etruscan art, Italy: Tomb of the Augurs, c.530 BCE. Copy of Tomb Painting. Ny Carlsberg Glypotek. Denmark. Courtesy of Getty Images

other words, the masked figure is understood to manage/control the meaning of what is seen. He makes meaning; he controls meaning. The mask manages or controls as it deflects and disrupts perception or what seems to be the real; he projects and communicates through and in spite of or in opposition to what the eyes and ears signal to be significance, implications, ramifications, meaning.[75] Meaning is mask-ed—not merely covered up or merely communicated, but made more profound and poignant, as it is "per-formed," made part of that world's system of "make-believe." The latter, in Napier and among many different theorists, goes beyond the issue of sincerity or the illusory or the delusional; it has to do with sensibilities about and orientation to doubt and uncertainty, to fear and anxiety, to the challenges and limitations of forms and types and degrees of knowing.[76] Channeling Gilbert Ryle in understanding "make-believe" to be "of a higher order than that of belief,"[77] Napier comes to accept the notion that human existence is essentially ordered around the make-believe once thought to be the province only of ritual and the theater. He comes to understand and argue that the "efficacy"—including greater agency and freedom and elasticity of thinking and knowing and orientation—of "make-believe" is evident as a distinct "advantage" across the domains of human life.[78]

But what are the problems and challenges, the "drawbacks" as Napier refers to them, in the epistemic economy of mask-ing? Napier identifies the obverse of the openness and freedom of make-believe as "the less than unanimous character of any justification for human action and the melancholic tendencies that result from ... the inability to know what force can be held accountable for a specific event."[79] This "uncertainty" or the "inability to ... know" is the chief shortcoming of the work of the masks. It would seem that constant and raised anxiety over uncertainty and fluidity and complexity and multiple sources of power—what some have called "polytheism"—disposes or makes the world vulnerable to (the claims to) certitude—what some have called "monotheism."

To be sure, with these two weighty categories—polytheism and monotheism—long and complex fraught histories are collapsed by Napier into radically simplistic abbreviations or handles, if not tortured thinking, but I beg consideration of the major point that he makes and that needs to be made here: At issue are modes/ways of knowing and making and communicating meaning and their politics. Given this interest, notwithstanding their clunkiness, the terms are apt handles that need to be made more discursively supple to register two distinct orientations to the world and to knowing and negotiating the world. Napier quotes historian of religion Huston Smith's rather astounding but hardly outlier sentiment in his well-regarded standard primer *Religions of Man* (1958) about what may be considered the chief problem or point of anxiety in the mask-ing society and culture:

> If man's life is not to be *scattered* [my emphasis], if he is not to spend his days darting from one cosmic bureaucrat to another to discover who is setting the *standards* today, if, in short, there is a consistent way in which life is to be lived if it is to move toward fulfillment, a way that can be searched out and approximated, there must be a *singleness* to the *Other* that supports this way.[80]

Although Napier does not elaborate, I suspect he was, like me, especially struck by "standards," "singleness," and "Other" (terms I have emphasized) in Smith's argument: In these terms are responses to a growing and palpable anxiety, an insecurity understood to define the mask-ing world. The fear expressed in Smith's use of another term—"scattered"—in regard to human life in general or a particular expression of social life captures rather poignantly Achebe's title and the story it announces. The scattered life cannot be far or different from the life in which things have fallen apart.

So we are brought back to Achebe's story about the world of Umuofia. I have tried to make the case that the latter must be seen to represent, among other things, a system of knowing. This system of knowing, in fact, was—I think it appropriate now to indicate—*managed* by and within a type of logic and tradition, a semiosphere,[81] what the readers—and perhaps even some villagers within the story—encounter as the surface part of a complex ritual. What was managed was a knowing that was male-ordered, male-focused, reflective of mostly male-specific anxieties and fears. Embedded within the "dance of the mask,"[82] the knowing that was constructed was seriously playful and playfully serious. Only (elite) males could know, so that—according to a disturbing politics and structure of logic—through them, the whole clan might know, and so be ordered.

No matter the personal levels and types of foibles and drama going on within Okonkwo in *TFA*, it is clear enough that most decisive for the fate of Umuofia—some foibles intersecting with Okonkwo, and some others going beyond him—were the developments in connection with the coming of the British. The latter's presence was decisive not so much in terms of their arms but as an alternate system of knowing, of communication and of orientation to the world that was tightly arranged and managed, closed and predictable. The representation of this difference was the undoing of Umuofia. Even if Okonkwo had, with the support of his fellows in the clan, routed the British, the fundamental problem involving defections would have remained. Things fell apart in Umuofia because the drive to know and to belong within such a system of certainty with certainty was offered by the British.

To be sure, masking and the dancing it inspired did not mean simply covering up, silencing, or hiding something or someone from view. Rather, it signaled complexity of ways of knowing, the difficulty of grasping and possessing knowledge, the necessity for collective negotiation and consideration. It signaled doubt that the apparent is the real, the stable truth. It communicates that the truth lies beyond the surface level or appearances, that the real is an "encompassing mystery that is inexhaustible."[83] Notwithstanding their invariance as part of ritual, the mask-ing dances ironically and profoundly perform contingency and variability—what I have termed scripturalectics, the set of arrangements and terms by which communication and knowing are established and managed, in its most basic form. That basic form is play, performance. In spite of the attempts to occlude the truth about this form, about the reality of construction, it endures. Such play made local societies the likes of Umuofia highly vulnerable to the rhetorics, unacknowledged performances, and politics of certainty that defined the extensive colonial world the likes of the British empire. To an accounting and ramifications of the development of the latter we turn in the next chapter.

CHAPTER 2

"PACIFICATION OF THE PRIMITIVE TRIBES"

MEANING AS WHITE SAVAGERY

> Reverend James Smith . . . saw things as black and white.
> And black was evil . . . the world was a battlefield in
> which the children of light were locked in moral conflict with the
> sons of darkness . . . He believed in slaying the prophets of Baal.
>
> —*Things Fall Apart, Chapter 22*

> [I]n every society the production of discourse is at once controlled,
> selected, organized and redistributed according to a certain number
> of procedures, whose role is to avert its powers and its dangers, to
> cope with chance events, to evade its ponderous, awesome materiality . . .
> We must conceive discourse as a violence that we do to things, or,
> at all events, as a practice we impose upon them; it is in this practice
> that the events of discourse find the principle of their regularity.
>
> —*Michel Foucault, "The Discourse on Language"*

"Pacification of the Primitive Tribes of the Lower Niger." These strange and now-haunting famous words are part of the last sentence of *TFA*. They constitute the title of the book the British colonial District Commissioner (DC) was at work on. The title is jarring, freighted, even a bit frightening. It is the book the DC intends to write about the natives in the region now being occupied and transformed by the British. The plan is for the book to include "material" about the ways of the Umuofian natives and to chronicle a particular example— mostly exemplary, of course, even with missteps here and there—of late-nineteenth/early-twentieth-century British colonial sub-Saharan African management styles and policies. The narrator makes the DC indicate what "point" in the book would be "stress[ed]": it would now include "new material" having to do with Okonkwo's suicide, his dangling from a tree (British delicacy of expression and avoidance of gaze), but it would be generally framed as a record of British "pacification" (wry British euphemy) of "primitives" (British-inflected racialism). That same material that was the tree and that was the facilitator of Okonkwo's death would also chillingly and poignantly provide the type of material for the writing of the book!

Pacification. Primitive Tribes. Book. Writing. These terms and related matters need to be further stressed here at the outset of this chapter.

Pacification as a term is an example of the now widely known, if not highly regarded, British understatement or euphemy. *Pacified?* *Who* might be pacified? Pacified by whom and to what end? The term surely masks contempt—of the British for the non-British, perhaps, but certainly for those dominated by the British. The term seems to be used to deflect and, perhaps, oddly, make it easier to experience the dominance that reflects if not inspires contempt. Most likely, the term is used both by dominants within the narrative and by Achebe himself to speak to the psychology of dominance, the psychology of the management of others. The regime is the British empire that had approached, within the narrative time of Achebe's story, its greatest extent of historical expansiveness.

Primitive tribes. Savages, anyone? The reasoning among those invading must be that only those who are backwards and without civilization can and should be managed. We know now that the ideology of modern antiblack racism was cultivated in the aftermath of the European slave trade. In the throes of the monstrous trade, notwithstanding all that it wrought in commercial terms and in the expansion of European capital(ism), it had to be rationalized. Naming and theorizing and ideologizing—signifying—the sub-Saharan black African enslaved as children, as retarded and backward peoples requiring European discipline and governance, was the way to explain and justify the trade. All those beyond Christianity were deemed savages; among such could be included some European tribes and Muslims and varieties of Asians, with their various religious traditions, some of

which were scriptural traditions that might be comparable to but ultimately, in the most important respects, were inferior to Christian traditions. Those outside European modernity and enlightenment were
deemed primitives. So exotic and benighted were they considered—
because they were without modern conventional writing traditions, for
example—that they were deemed doubly cursed.[1]

The book. And writing. And reading. This is what distinguishes the
higher from the lower, civilization from existence as primitives. The
book is the technology by which dominance is effected and extended,
how transcendence is established and maintained. With the book,
after all, the Christian god is found and engaged and is everywhere all-
powerful. Seen clearly enough by the stranger, the outsider—including
the complexly oriented narrator of the story—the book is for the
British (and Europeans, more generally) a "fetish." Associated with it
is power, "magic," to effect all sorts of outcomes, in addition to the
"government" of local native peoples.

It is the book (and reading/writing) that best represents the presence and power of the British. It is a stand-in for British networks and
systems of communication in the most general terms. As it was experienced on the ground—among the locals—it was mostly, although
not exclusively, the Bible that was at issue. It is clearly the Bible that
Achebe made the major site of controversy in *TFA*: Missionaries were
depicted as being among the front-line soldiers in the empire's advance
in Africa and beyond. Their defensive and offensive weapon was the
Bible. It was made to signify the mysterious power of the British. How
otherwise to explain their power to lure locals away from their traditions? How otherwise to account for their powers of healing? How to
explain their claims to know about so many things? How to understand their very presence in Umuofia?

Throughout *TFA* the Bible is featured as a site or sign of British
power as well as a window through which to see British facilitation
and contestation and recording of, and befuddlement over, Umuofia's
"falling apart." The narrative turn to the appearance of white men—
"The missionaries had come to Umuofia" (83)—is registered most dramatically in terms of the appearance and uses of the Bible.

The strange men are heard making outrageous statements and strange claims that even typical translation challenges and the particular awkwardnesses of the local situation could not address or overcome, notwithstanding the narrator's offices. Umuofians were told about "this new God, the Creator of all the world and all the men and women." They were also told in terms of great certainty[2] that Umuofians worshipped "false gods, gods of wood and stone." In spite of the disturbing response—"A deep murmur went through the crowd"—the harangues continued. Umuofians were strongly exhorted to "leave your wicked ways and false gods and turn to Him so that you may be saved." That this rhetoric is clearly biblical in origins and in intonation—even as it is over a long period of time a composite of different sources here and there and has gone through subsequent historical cultural translations and permutations, the most recent of which would be that associated with the Victorian era—is without question.[3] It is the source known by the missionaries that provides the air of authority. Questions and counterarguments do not prevail. Which god is the god referenced? "There is only one true God" (84). A breathtaking claim! But even more breathtaking is the degree to which we have come/been made to accept it as natural, far from outrageous.

The narrator has little need to name explicitly or have any characters point out the source of authority (or arrogance) in evidence. Biblical references are embedded in the rhetorics of the British missionaries to the point of appearing not to be separate from their persons. The Bible not only is conveyed in apodictic statements but is also embedded in the hymns taught the locals (85). In response to questions raised about any subject or issue—even those far beyond "religion"—answers are provided that are themselves reflective of absolutist biblical rhetorics. After the missionaries—"crazy men"—had spent some time among villagers, saying and doing many things that "puzzled," the narrator summed up the generally held view of them: "that the white man's fetish had unbelievable power" (86). There should be little doubt that here, with the term "fetish," Achebe is signifying on—capping on, reversing—white men's already long history of marking Africans as "primitives" peculiarly subject to the fetishizing of objects.[4] The object that need not be named here is the white men's book, "the Bible," "the scriptures," "the Word of God." It was generally agreed, even taken for granted among "white men"—certainly, the white men who were the British—that through such an object God spoke and made things happen. Indeed, all books were more or less thought to be significant. Therein lies their "unbelievable power"—insofar as they projected in association with the book such unprecedented certainty and confidence: "There is only one true God" (84); "worship the true God" (87). Period.

The book that was the Bible was itself part—the most important part, to be sure—of a larger system, what might be thought about in terms of a language system or regime. This system is what I am calling scripturalization. That Achebe thought along these general lines is evident in his Chapter 18, in which he again summarized developments surrounding the coming of the British. At this point he made the case—a bit strained and strange, but nonetheless relevant and poignant—that stories had circulated among villagers that the white man "had not only brought a religion but also a *government*" (89; emphasis mine). I take this term to capture Achebe's understanding of how encompassing—captivating!—was the influence of the British in the life of the village of Umuofia. "Religion" was not enough to capture the radical changes wrought by the British "presence." The change was already—from the perspective of the narrator—multidimensional, sedimented, deep, far-reaching, felt in every sector of life. "Government"—"white man's government"— captured the capture (89, again on 99).

The establishment of "white man's government" in Umuofia (and all that for which Umuofia was a stand-in) was accomplished primarily not through warfare but "quietly," via the more devastatingly powerful psycho-socio-cultural influence. And the latter was effected primarily through "religion," which was made transcendent—that is, was transported through the agency of scriptures (viz., *things written*) as the political and as social-cultural power. The "only true Word of God." Such power was in evidence in every domain of life—from "religion" to commerce to the courts, and in the individual's and the corporate body's head. When Obierika and Okonkwo together mourn the loss of the village and its traditions to the white men and their ways, Obierika in response to Okonkwo's incredulity and shock over this development points to how this was accomplished:

> ... our own brothers who have taken up his religion also say that our customs are bad. How do you think we can fight when our own brothers have turned against us? The white man is very clever. He came *quietly* and *peaceably* with his *religion*. We were amused at his foolishness and allowed him to stay. Now he has won our brothers, and our clan can no longer act like one. He has put a knife on the things that held us together and we have *fallen apart*. (100)

This assault on the traditional was far-reaching and profound and elicited a note of the ironic. The "falling apart" was in evidence no matter the attitude or discretionary policies of the white men, encountered as missionaries or as commissioners. It happened under the more severe policies of the hardliner the Rev. Mr. Smith, but it also happened with the relatively moderate attitudes and policies of the missionary Mr. Brown. When a fanatical convert named Enoch "murdered"— unmasked—an *egwugwu*, the decision was made to retaliate by burning down the white men's "shrine." Mr. Smith "stood his ground" against the threat and the eventual actual burning of the church. And when the *egwugwu* retreated as though satisfied that with the retaliatory burning the assault had been curtailed, the narrator, in concluding his report about this incident, suggested that "for the moment" the clan was "pacified" (108).

But the term is strikingly at odds with common sense, and with gut feelings. The reader knows—is made to feel strongly—that this cannot possibly be the end of the story. It feels rather like the beginning of something shaky, if not horrible, something to make one ill at ease. Things were far from being at peace. The clan had not been pacified. White men with such power could not possibly be turned around or routed in this way. There was an unquiet about the quiet. Okonkwo was "almost happy" with the villagers' response—heroic, aggressive, in his view—to what the church represented. But everyone was on edge—and armed. Skirmishes and conflict continued. The DC was involved and threatened punishment—"justice"—in the name of "the queen, the most powerful ruler in the world." The decision: He apprehended six ruling members of the clan who had gathered to address the situation and levied against them a fine, two hundred bags of cowries. The fine was paid. "Okonkwo was choked with hate." It was his undoing. He ground his teeth. He swore vengeance (113).

Okonkwo was determined to take action. He met with other elders about the situation. At Okonkwo's compound, "in a flash," he killed a messenger who had been sent by the DC to inform all gathered to cease and desist. Confusion ensued. Okonkwo fled. When the dust had settled and the DC had arrived on the scene, Okonkwo's body was found behind his compound "dangling" from a tree (117).

In response to the request from Obierika for assistance in handling the body, the DC, knowing Okonkwo's death had put an end to the acute tension and conflict, then became a "student"—of "primitive customs." This turn, or better, perhaps, this window onto British colonial rule, is critical: It shows how the rule is established and maintained—mostly in connection with writing. Not only is writing the means by which colonial rule communicates with and takes direction from, the metropole, it is also the means by which "primitives" are "pacified." This latter term is significant. It takes us back to the valences of the term I discussed above and the reference to the term earlier in the story: There was fateful, almost haunting, irony in the "pacification" that ensued in the wake of the assault on the white men's church or shrine. Such "peace" was fleeting. In the wake of Okonkwo's suicide, as all things had clearly fallen apart for Umuofia, there is another eerie peace that is referenced—the type easily assumed on the part of the DC to obtain firmer grasp and for a long period. This is the peace that was colonial rule. The pacification meant here has to do with ruling primitives, keeping them in order. It is from the perspective of the narrator a fraught and cynical and bitter peace. And it is maintained, even as it is by Achebe chillingly and disturbingly announced, by writing.

It is the association of pacification with writing that, for the interests and focus of this book, begs attention. It is writing and its projection (and fetishization) in the book that is made to do the work of managing the Umuofians (and all others whom they represent, within and beyond *TFA*). As is indicated in the rhetorically economic terms that are Achebe's story, pacification-as-management is accomplished by naming, defining, overdetermining, and circumscribing the Umuofians. They are first of all pronounced "*primitives*." And they are *enscripturalized*[5]—made to be what they are on account of being written up in the records in papers and books. The latter are essentially made a weapon of assault against the Umuofians. These people are through language inscribed and invented as an ironically alien people, for the sake of British rule. And given the reach and perdurance, the fixity of writing, the inscription and invention would remain, notwithstanding independence.[6]

The phenomenon of what now can only be understood in terms of the ironic and sardonic pacification in relationship to the Umuofians—and beyond, or more generally throughout the colonial regime—works on at least two different planes. First, as we have already seen, there are the scriptures, understood in the narrow terms of the object employed or manipulated by the missionaries. The latter carried and employed (and deployed)—read from, pointed out, projected, quoted from, paraphrased—the English Bible as scriptures as advancement not only of the strictly religious-evangelical but also simultaneously and coextensively the broader socio-cultural-economic-political colonial formation agenda. There was no simple or honest way or reason for Achebe and his contemporary cohorts who shared his sensibilities and political commitments to separate out the different agenda among different social-cultural and political groups and interests that defined and contributed to the big agenda of the colonial project. Thus, the word "scriptures" in Umuofia and throughout the English world was also shorthand, understood and used to refer to writing in general, books, other documents/texts/colonial schooling and communication in general. In the other more pointed, perhaps disturbing, words—those of Olaudah Equiano—as I have indicated, scriptures represented "white men's magic." As such, scriptures captured not only the politics and practices of the colonials but also the terms around which the colonized and enslaved engaged in complex mimetics.

The dynamics that obtained between the Umuofians and the British in Achebe's story (and in his own actual historical experience) also obtained between others who—before and during and beyond the historical setting for his story (that is, in the early modern era)—were among the dispossessed and colonized and enslaved persons of the world who were of black African ancestry and other white men. But it seems that nothing throws into relief the origins, development, and consequences of the dynamics that from reading Equiano I call "white men's magic," what Achebe called "pacification," what in this book is analyzed more deeply and broadly in terms of the phenomenon of scripturalization in modern-world history.

I should like below to discuss briefly examples that, like Achebe's story of the Umuofians, represent what was and continues to be at stake. Their importance lies in the wide analytical windows they open onto the occluded and occluding work of scripturalization. But before these examples are discussed I should like to provide a general interpretive framework for scripturalization through use of a powerful image as a springboard for thinking about the sort of mentality—of denial and disavowal in the face of the humanity of the other; the fear and anxiety generated by contact with the other—that frames the whole period in which blacks (and other nonwhite peoples) and the Europeans who have become white peoples are brought into "contact." As has been argued before, through such contact, black peoples, especially, are signified and troped by Europeans. Through such interpretive work black peoples are seen as challenges and problems, as deficits and subhumans. This signifying/troping is accomplished through the phenomenon and politics of scripturalization.

I now turn again[7] to a provocative image-example (see Figure 1.1) that throws a complex phenomenon into relief: the frontispiece to Lafitau's ethnological work. But here the focus is placed on the process of scripturalization itself as part of consolidation of empire. Earlier, it was enough to indicate that, in spite of Lafitau's projections, the villagers in Achebe's story-world moved, danced, sang, and spoke to and for themselves. The work that Lafitau's image was doing or aimed to do did not matter much in that discussion. Because in this chapter the focus is on how that work was effected a bit more explanation is required.

Note again that the gendered but otherwise unmarked (viz., *unra-cialized* [European white]) inscriber/historian of the world and inter-preter of events and truth transcendent, seated with pen and paper, looks up. She is complexly situated—in close proximity to and appar-ently directly gazing at the anthropomorphized Father Time and Death (and attendants). The Father Time figure points her to the image in the image—of the past, the European invention and image of the ancient world, with its social order, including pagans, barbar-ians, and believers. She writes within and for the larger framework that is Europe ascendant. But she must write in order to clarify, in light of the "contact" made with the Others and the changes that have ensued in the world, how things, in light of the past, now must *mean*. Notice that along the bottom of the image there are objects, trinkets, fetishes, belonging to and representing the Others. The History, the Truth that is to be told about these "savages" and "primitives" must now be told in the terms of the method of bricolage—assembling, choosing this and that part, this or that thing, from this or that world of savagery—in order to place the Others within the framework. The latter is represented by the image on the wall reflecting the strategi-cally important Manichaean psychology and epistemics of the colonial order. The "savage" is assumed not to be able to communicate, at least not in "purified" language, so deserves no hearing and demands no respectful gaze, no serious attention. Yet this Other must be inscribed into the new reality and interpreted and interpellated. The Other is scripturalized into existence and made/allowed to mean in a particular way, given names and characteristics.

I should like to turn to the question that begs consideration here—about the kind of world that is presumed to be under construction and ordered in the Lafitau image. Such a world must be assumed to be roundly, if not comprehensively and absolutely, scripturalized. This does not mean universal literacy, but it does mean that in such a world power is inherent in or turns around uses of conventional literacy. And it is understood that this system of knowing and communication, the uses of language and discourse, must be consistently, heavily, policed or managed. In his *L'écriture de l'histoire* (*Writing of History*), De Certeau makes eighteenth-century France a strong example of precisely this point—that this world came to be "managed" (*policé*) through the structuring of language and religion, religion as language. These two categories in functional terms become one domain, one sphere of control and manipulation. The clerics come to be socialized as the functionaries—the living embodiment, carriers, guarantors of the right order—of a religious system or ideology. They were in this era committed to getting right—even living, reflecting—the interpretation of the defining texts (scriptures) and the practices and rites the texts called for. They saw themselves responsible for the management of doctrine, ritual, and all other pertinent practices that mark the church now as structure.[8]

A certain ideologization of practices for the sake of the organization, consolidation, and control of the (French) state in this period stressed the need to govern "social nature," the emotions and beliefs of all subjects. *Gouverner, c'est faire croire* ("To govern is to make subjects believe")—so went what was understood to be the animating ideological principle under Richelieu and Louis XIII.[9] De Certeau indicates that the philosopher Marin Mersenne, of the same general period, is said to have argued rather bluntly the "management of minds" as the overarching rational goal of the state.[10]

De Certeau's almost cursory unelaborated reference to Nicolas de la Mare's second book (Livre II) of his famous *Traité de la Police* (1705) belies its importance. Devoted to religion as *"le premier & le principal objet de la Police"* ("the first and principal object of governance"), this second book makes dramatic the point not only that policing of society and culture in general was for elites at issue, but that "religion" in particular, first and foremost, was to be policed and to function as police, and that this policing would be done through manipulation and control *of* discourse, manipulation and control *as* discourse (*Premieres preuves tirees de l'Ecriture Sainte, des Conciles, des Peres & du Droit Canon*).[11] In other words, religion was partly—for the sake of serving the interests of the new nationalist and nationalizing elites—(re)constructed as discourse, specifically in terms of the scriptural (broadly defined). In this regime, clerics were oriented differently: They began to function no longer on the traditional order of shamans and priests, but as scholars and exegetes, "living scriptures," defenders of the language of dominance against non-Catholics and the religio-social-culturally impious.[12]

If we fast-forward to the late nineteenth century—a period closer to, arguably the historical backdrop for, the situation Achebe describes in *TFA*—we can see some of the dramatic and disturbing and perduring consequences of the ideologization of Europeanist mind management in what can be considered the advancement of nationalization—on the order that we recognize today. There is also a correlative development in what I should like to consider cultural-ideological production, at once reflecting and further supporting and consolidating nationalization.

Consider what is now known as the Berlin Conference, the Congo Conference, or the Scramble for Africa, of 1884–1885 (Figure 2.1). Convened by Otto von Bismarck, the meeting was intended to divide Africa according to the interests—social, political, and economic—of the European powers at the time. Never has Europe been so united, so much in agreement. In this case it was in much agreement around the (re)drawing of boundaries, the (re)naming of peoples of another part of the world, and the subjection of such peoples to different (European) languages and customs, rules and laws. The conference ushered in a period of fevered activity resulting in a period of colonial rule, disruption, and violence that obtained on most terms until well into the twentieth century, with the onset of the independence movements. Other aspects of the conference agreement continue to have their effects to this day.

The major point to be made here is that Africa was, through the conference, signified. More to the point, it was scripturalized; written

Figure 2.1 "The Congo Conference in Berlin." Wood engraving after a drawing by Adalbert von Rößler (1853–1922). From *Überland und Meer,* vol. 53, 1883/85.

up according to the interests of this or that state; inscribed as ("new," almost "modern") peoples in subject relationship to other peoples. The (different types of) scripturalizations of the French peoples, of the British, and so forth, provided the ideological and political conditions for the (en)scripturalization (what Achebe terms the pacification) of the black Others. Those who cannot be placed or cannot place themselves within, or negotiate, the scriptural regime around which the (European-defined) nation is constructed and defined are considered and engaged as Other, as marginal, with the severest consequences. The possibilities for humiliation and subjection of the Other are wide-ranging and consequential. Those who cannot "read" (the nation, culture) cannot hope to be counted or countenanced.

At about the same time as the dynamics pertaining to the Berlin Conference there was an example of high social-cultural production that was also reflective and constructive of the fraught times.

As incredible as it may seem—especially to U.S. readers—I have in mind a scholarly production: the politics and social psychology that obtained with the publication of the project that the famous philologist/Sanskritist F. Max Müller (1823–1900) supervised and edited and called *Sacred Books of the East*.[13] This enormous and complex work, 50 volumes in total, produced during the fraught years 1879 to 1910, the period of the height of colonialist expansion and violence, both reflected and determined much about how peoples—especially the Anglophones, but I think also much of the North Atlantic—would come to understand and negotiate the world. It reflected and modeled and consolidated what I now call the ideology of *scripturalism* and scripturalization as its projection as a discursive regime over the modern world.

Billed as a collection of the "sacred texts" of the world—scandalously excepting the books of the Jewish-Christian religion as those books not to be categorized and interrogated on the same terms—Müller's project firmly consolidated and legitimized what he called the "aristocracy of the book religion." And he made clear the framing agenda of dominance and violence of his project captured in his own description of his work—collapsing the classification of religion and the classification of language and culture and races—in his use of the old premodern world expression *dividé et impera*. The expression was shockingly but bluntly and honestly translated by him as "classify and conquer." That the ideology and politics behind this expression could have been spoken or thought about at the Berlin Conference is easily imagined; the one project or initiative enabled or facilitated the other. The inventions, the new realities—language- or discourse-based—were all worked on and worked out around the (clerk's or) scholar's desk.[14]

So regarding Müller's project, we see the agenda here: The Christian West's books are not to be classified, not to be the focus of critical inquiry, not to be excavated or interrogated, alongside other traditions, such as Islam, Hinduism, Buddhism. These latter traditions were to be compared to Christianity in connection with the project and (re) invented along the lines of Christian tradition—but as inferior versions of such. Like whiteness itself in the modern world, Christianism, or the unstable, extended, constructed, fraught, complex Jewish-Christianism, was not to be interrogated or even acknowledged on the same terms as all the other books (that is, as sites for critical exploration). These traditions were to be bracketed, to be treated differently, to be exegeted, their content-truths decoded (but only by certified/authorized clerics—academic or high cultural).[15]

This sort of cultural practice and its politics—of naming/marking—marks where we live and the times in which we live. It suggests consolidation or an advanced state of scripturalization, in this case in narrow terms, or on the social-cultural track, albeit with ramifications aplenty for nationalization. The production of the Sacred Books anthology clearly suggests the collapse of religion into textualization, with all that this means in terms of (the politics of) constriction of engagement and legitimate cultural practice and political practice and power. It squares with what is set up and being taught in the scripturalized academy: the study of (legitimate, publicly sanctioned) religion construed as the study of texts. Sanctioned religion is scriptural religion. And there are sanctioned rules about the study of such. Using the Sacred Books project as touchstone, as one important marker, I contend that we now sojourn in the time of the consolidation of the ideology of *scripturalism* and the social-cultural-political regimes of *scripturalization*. New technologies or new media do not upend the ideology or the regime; the capacity for accommodation and cooptation is evident throughout history.[16]

We have hardly begun the hard work of taking stock of what it means to be situated in such a world, whether we call it by my term, scripturalization/scripturalism, or following Marshall McLuhan, the "Gutenberg Galaxy."[17] That there has hardly been a reconsideration or deep or sustained criticism of this development can be seen in the recent publication of the 4,000-plus-page *Norton Anthology of World Religions*, edited by Jack Miles (along with a collective of established scholars in various fields and traditions).[18] Hailed in reviews as magisterial and authoritative, the project is pretty much for the first part of the twentieth century confirmation and consolidation of what Müller's late-nineteenth-century colonialist project represented. Its claim to broader representativeness (of "religions") in my view hardly makes it less problematic in conceptual-political terms. For the "globalized" twentieth century—with its mounting evidence of the extent and nature of the havoc wrought by and challenges to the scripturalizations of the Berlin Conference—it is arguably far more problematic in its very existence and conceptualization and apparent obliviousness to what it represents. How can this canon-consolidating project not extend the (discursivity of the) colonial order?

It was in an early phase of such a world of scripturalization that the dynamics of the story that Achebe tells unfolded. In this world things fall apart for whatever internal infrapolitical reasons, to be sure, but clearly also on account of the scriptural politics advanced, in this instance, by the British. What is so important about the story Achebe tells is that it is told from the perspective—complex, to be sure (how could it not be?)—of some among those being signified/scripturalized. He shows readers how some characters wrestle against the odds that scripturalization represents. His work involves projecting complexity of perspective and positionality, with degrees of self-reflexivity and splitness. In this respect, Achebe's story is part of rich and heroic if sometimes belated efforts among the modern subaltern that are African/African diaspora peoples to speak and write/back—to empires. It is a complex registration of sentiment and perspective: To see, to hear from, to read the sentiments of the scripturalized is counterintuitive and against tradition and history. Herein lies an aspect or part of the power of Achebe's work.

The examples that follow show how, in different situations and domains, scripturalization was refracted in different domains and contexts, with windows opened onto how the dominated experienced and further shaped (our perspectives of) the phenomenon.

As I have already indicated briefly, I include as one of the poignant, even defining, examples of the phenomenon of modern-world scripturalization Olaudah Equiano's story about himself and the worlds (British and European and Euro-American) he had to negotiate. Aspects of his story that are pertinent to scripturalization I have already discussed to some length in *WMM*. The latter, with the focus on the conceptualization of the phenomenon of scripturalization, is inspiration and touchstone for this book, but there are more questions and issues to be explored. Equiano's telling of his story, including his own play with scriptures, provides a fascinating historical example (I argue it is one of the most fascinating, certainly disturbing examples) of African diaspora mimetics of scriptures, scripturalizing, and scripturalization. This is for me the point of making Equiano's story if not the central point, then the backdrop or textured example, the social-cultural analytical palette on and in relationship to which the fuller picture and story can be told: Equiano signifies on the (European or North Atlantic cultural) signifying that has to do with scriptures/scripturalizing/scripturalization. He shows scripturalization as power; he shows it to be violent, tragic. His story is an attempt to make it mostly about how the British inflection of scripturalization was "donated" to him, how he embodies it, uses it, plays with it, suffers from it. As always, the question is about the degree to which one is ensnared in the play, in the trap laid for others. At any rate, my ongoing fascination with Equiano's story is a reflection of my conviction that what it, among other things, points us to—the expansive valences of scriptures in terms of mimetics—remains a challenge and opportunity to any effort to explain how black peoples came to negotiate and survive European worlds. Given its rich texture and its disturbing twists and turns, I shall also want to make further use of Equiano's story as part of the effort to analyze scripturalization as a type of enslavement as well as an opportunity for negotiation, accommodation, exercise of agency, assumption and use of voice.

But for the moment another historical situation—historically prior to, perhaps more emotionally wrenching than, even if not as broadly ramifying as that of, Equiano's—will open another window onto an example of scripturalization as a wedge into the political agenda and dynamics of "pacification." The situation is heartrending insofar as it casts light on the darkness of scriptural play. From an earlier seventeenth-century setting, this story of the erasure of a black female charismatic evangelical figure in the mix of dynamics having to do with the Great Revolution will, with its focus on the exegetical-hermeneutical violence that obtained, provide a riveting and disturbing example of how scripturalization was accomplished and with what effects. That is, how the violence in this instance is done directly to an individual, by the name of Francis, ostensibly for the sake of a certain politics of religious formation. That this individual was black and female is all the more to the point about the breadth and depths of the effects on subalterns as well as the motoring interests and agenda of dominants.

But first, a broad background view of the worlds being formed and the dynamics in play is in order. A glimpse of Equiano's world in mid- to late-eighteenth-century Britain and what it suggested was at issue in regard to scripturalization provides a historical-conceptual bridge. Then we go back in time to the world that Francis helped shape, even as she was scripturally rendered invisible and silent in it.

Equiano's story reflects an awareness of and a creative response to the mid- to late-eighteenth-century situation that was itself an explosive response of activism to the legacy of the previous centuries of European internal social-political and religion-inflected conflict. The eighteenth was also the century of the development of more extensive and complex international commerce and trade, including slave-trafficking as a significant part of the underpinning of such, all of which had as collateral impact the toxicity that was increasing anti-black racialist rhetorics and racialist ideologization as rationalization and legitimation. Equiano's activism, in association with many other individuals and groups, as reflected in the letters and petitions to which he was signatory, if not also instigator and author, was a response to the increase in volume—and shrillness—of "scientific" and literary and religious discourses about race, racial origins, and racial hierarchy. Few persons of the period, certainly few non-Europeans finding themselves involuntarily located in Europe and in European colonies, would be unaware of such discourses and rhetorics and politics, and their direct ramifications. "Strangers"—non-Europeans recently "discovered" and dominated—were obviously directly affected in all sorts of negative ways. These minoritized persons could not fail to notice that in social locations ranging from the universities to palaces and parliaments to churches and taverns and debating halls, they were the focus of discussions and debates and scholarly inquiry. They were very much aware that they were overdetermined in European discourses. They were aware of how they ranked in the logic and regime of the new racial hierarchializations among Europeans, colonizers or not. In the Europeans' new ideological schema, inspired by the "discovery" of the Others, captured most vividly in the notion of the "Great chain of being," blacks were clearly at the bottom; they were popularly and devastatingly deemed, as Peter Linebaugh and Marcus Rediker noted in their fascinating book *The Many-Headed Hydra: Sailors, Slaves, Commoners, and the Hidden History of the Revolutionary Atlantic* (2000), "hewers of wood and drawers of water."[19] Given such a determination, black life would be precarious and experienced as constant humiliation and stress, if not always violence.

The larger historical backdrop of black humiliation as Equiano and his black contemporaries experienced it in Britain is in the early to middle seventeenth century. This was a period of tremendous social and political upheaval and revolution throughout the North Atlantic worlds, especially in what became Britain, in which, in a fascinating period, "variously designated dispossessed commoners, transported felons, indentured servants, religious radicals, pirates, urban labourers, soldiers, sailors, and African slaves," along with some women who crossed many of these categories, made common cause to a degree and for a limited time, as some contemporaries viewed it, as a monstrous and threatening "many-headed hydra."[20] A further historical background note should be taken of some aspects of this period in order to gain perspective not only on what Equiano experienced and what he perceived and reacted to, but also on what may have informed Achebe's story.[21] (For the discussion that follows I continue to draw from Linebaugh and Rediker.)

Since the beginnings of English colonial expansion in the seventeenth century, the powerful had been given to referring to the myth involving Hercules and the hydra as a way to describe the challenges of imposing "order" on the new mixed global rabble of laborers. The colonizers were cast as Hercules, the rabble as the hydra. The use of the myth in this period expressed the fear in the new situation—fear that the volatility might bring chaos and disaster.

While the socioculturally and economically powerful, for some obvious reasons, tended to lump together all the non-powerful as constant potential threats to their position and to the situation—the "swinish multitude," as Edmund Burke put it[22]—it is both fascinating and chilling to note that among the non-elites, who imagined themselves radical transformers of the already transformed world, blacks were singled out as outcasts, as signs of evil, the all-too-convenient discursive symbol to reflect the problematics of black identity and aspirations in the new context.[23]

A disturbing example is found in John Bunyan, then and even now in many circles the famous icon of European religious radicalism. Known among the "roarers," "ranters," "bell-ringers," and "soldiers" in opposition to establishment government, church, and society, converted by a woman who led him to membership into one of those radical female-directed independent, non-Establishment religious formations, Bunyan became the most famous figure of this diverse and far-flung movement. Yet on the other side of the revolutionary period, his somewhat nostalgic millenarian writings also reflected and nurtured a rather virulent strain of antiblack rhetoric. In his famous heavily allegorical work *Pilgrim's Progress* (1678), blacks were made to figure sin and evil, the antagonist of the Christian. The protagonist Christian encountered "a man black of flesh," who "flattereth his Neighbour [and] spreadeth a Net for his feet."[24] Christiana, wife of Christian, met "the vile person" who, like the Ethiopian referred to in the Bible, "can never be washed clean."[25] In a poem for children Bunyan described and contrasted Moses as a "fair and comely" to his wife, "a swarthy Ethiopian."[26] In his war memoirs (*The Holy War* [1682]), Bunyan includes an allegory as ideological register that reverses and undermines the historical truth about colonial violence:

> Well, upon a time there was one Diabolus, a mighty Gyant, made an
> assault upon this famous Town of Mansoul, to take it, make it his

habitation. This Gyant was King of the Blacks or Negroes, and most raving Prince he was.[27]

What might we make of Bunyan, this hero of radical (English) protestant evangelicalism? What of his rhetorical moves? What of his consciousness and politics in the use of an allegorical-symbolization system that makes use of blackness in this way—that is, in a racialized, specifically antiblack, ideology in advancement of a radically absolutist and polarized piety? Why were black peoples figured as evil at the expense of solidarity with them as co-dissenters, among those who were ex-centrics and critics of the center? What was the chief logic or motivation for the antiblack figuration? Where was the fault line, if it was not at the point of faith or outsider status? Was this rhetoric simply a matter of lazily falling back upon centuries-old tropes for the sake of advancing and sharpening a religiocultural polarity? If not, what should we make of throwing real black peoples under the rhetorical bus for the sake of sharpening such polarity?[28] Whatever the motive, the result surely was a more explicit ideological whitening of (English) Christianity. Such rhetorical practice led all too easily to the fateful confusion of evangelical piety and existence with being white, sin with being black.[29]

Lest the example of Bunyan's rhetorics be understood as too handy and convenient a critical target, somehow atypical of European sentiments about black peoples and about race and racism during the period—merely a matter of rhetoric run wild, of allegorizing run amok—I turn to another example, one closer to the point to make about and the perspective to bring to Achebe's story and to the matter of the phenomenon of pacification as scripturalization, pacification as scripturalization. This example is from the same historical period and is also included in Linebaugh and Rediker's volume.

It is the story, as I indicated above, of a black woman named Francis. As a religious radical ("Anabaptist"), an independent and outspoken woman, and a black ("West Indian"), in one person she was a triple threat or triple problem in the minds of those who were fearful of the hydrarchy, the monstrosity of social change. Her story—or the part of her story that can be stitched together from the one complexly tendentious source left about her—makes the powerful case about how strong and pervasive, how basic and sedimented, just how real was the structure of what I term scripturalization, how powerfully ramifying it was in the con-fusion of Christian faith and whiteness. That this was the case within the radical evangelical subculture of seventeenth-century England should be noted as our current situation in the world in terms of racial hierarchializations and religious fundamentalisms is inventoried and analyzed. These subcultures are not flat and monocultural and apolitical; they are in fact, if nothing else, politically charged and dynamic, the sites of much social experimentation, for powerful if not always lasting good and ill. How did we come to accept the hierarchies as natural? Why are these hierarchies so persistent, nearly impossible to disturb and upend? One can hear across the centuries and borders the collective sighs of sadness over this situation.

There is the one freighted flint of a source available about "a Blackymore Maide Named Francis" of mid-seventeenth-century England. We know about this woman only through the writing of Edward Terrill, an elder of one of those female-inspired "radical religious congregations" that had emerged from the revolutionary period. As part of his explicitly apologetic and nostalgic history of the church—*The Records of a Church of Christ in Broadmead, Bristol, 1640–1678*[30] (later formed and called a Baptist church)—Terrill, drawing upon his various selected written sources and oral histories, including those from interviews with founder Dorothy Hazzard, made a brief but significant reference to Francis. First, I think it worth noting that no other name is given her, only the demeaning, overdetermining "Blackymore." It is likely that "Francis" was referred to by the (fictive) "family" of congregants as "sister"—possibly even as "mother." (It is also likely that, given her status in the world of whites, no name other than that which registered for her servile status in the white world was at hand. This loss of her real name was already a sign of her dispossession in the world.) That Terrill, writing as a member of the fictive "family," did not bring himself to describe her in this way speaks loudly, in anticipation of a problem to which the critical reader-interpreter must be alert. To whom was he writing? For what cause, that sister/mother Francis should be referred to in such a manner? Francis was obviously an important member of the circle; "pillar" is a word often used to refer to such persons. In the telling of the story of the congregation, this "one Memmorable member" very likely could not have been overlooked if Terrill wanted his "history" to be considered to any degree honest or complete. At any rate, Terrill made Francis serve his writing agenda.

Also referred to by Terrill as a "servant," as an "Ethyopian," as "this poor Aethiopian" (in bold in the original), Francis was certainly nonetheless in Terrill's "record"[31]—if not in other individual memories— kept in her place, very much overdetermined as an inferior, even as she was, perhaps because she was, according to Terrill, much beloved. No doubt part of what was at issue was the handling of the truth about Francis's conversion experience and powerful charismatic and spiritual leadership, including her office of "exhortation." This truth could not be altogether denied or erased from the record, but for certain reasons, it had to be managed, nuanced, spun, carefully script-ed:

> she gave greate ground for Charity to believe she was truly brought over to Christ ... and she walked very humble and blamelesse in her Conversation, to her end; and when she was upon her death bed: She sent a Remarkable Exhortation unto ye
>
> whole Church with whom she walked, as her last request unto them: which argued her holy, childlike fear of ye Lord; and how precious the Lord was to her Soule; as was observed by the manner of her Expressing it. Which was this, one of the Sisters of ye congregation coming to visit her, in her Sicknesse, She solemnly took her leave of her, as o this world; and pray'd ye sister, to rember her to ye whole congregation, and to tell them, that she did Begg every soule, To take heed that they did lett **The glory of God to be dear unto them** a word meet for ye Church ever to remember; and for every member to observe, that they doe not loose ye gory of God in their families, neighbourhoods or places where God casts them: it being ye dyeing words of a Blackmoore, fir for

a White heart to store. After which this Aethiopian yielded up ye Spirit to Jesus that redeemed her and was Honourably Interred being carried by ye Elders & ye chiefest of note of ye Brethren un ye Congregation (Devout men bearing her) to ye grave . .[32]

It was not enough for Terrill simply to describe Francis's power and the congregation's esteem and love for her. He included what are likely some of her words, probably as remembered by some within the circle.[33] The emphasis that he placed (bold in his text) on "The glory of God to be dear unto them" as among the likely final words of sister Francis (ostensibly communicated to another sister) reflects his recognition of her prophetic offices and powers. But, again, he needed to put his spin on this situation. That spin drew upon the Bible—selected rhetorics from which were used for ongoing formation. At the very end of the focus on Francis, in an effort to make certain that "this poor Aethiopian" would nonetheless be put into proper—official, canonical—perspective for the (later) reader "in our days":

> By this in our days, we may see, Experimentally, that Scripture made good, *oux est proso poleptes ho theos. Alla en panti ethnei*, that God is no respecter of faces: But among all nations, &. Acts 10:34:35

The normal English translation of the Greek *poleptes* is "persons," not "faces," as Terrill has it. This translation is incredible: Using "faces" as the translation draws attention to physical features—to sister Francis's black face—as a sign of the status of her humiliation in the larger dominant white world.[34] Terrill seemed to need to remind the reader that sister Francis was after all a "blackamoor," with no real status, no rights, no privileges appertaining therewith. The point surely was to readjust the focus—from the radical view of Francis as "sister," as equal, within the church circle, with relativization of differences of color and race and gender in what was considered fealty to primitive Christian orientations and ideals, to a view (his own, but surely also representing others in his circle in time) in which her otherness is reestablished and highlighted and made to serve the infra-cultural apologetic interests of a congregation now to be defined by and centered around whites and whiteness even while projecting interests simply otherworldly.

Francis (and her kind) came to be troped (away); her membership in the circle of believers was now deemed by Terrill and his (real and imagined) associates to be a dramatic fulfillment of scriptures, insofar as she was black-faced: "God is no respecter of" difference. Never mind that sister Francis was not so much that one whose presence was testimony to the heavenly outlook of his circle; she was actually very likely one of the founding and dynamic and defining forces of the congregation. She was a pillar, not a commercial for evangelical growth and establishment. That the congregation, looking back through Terrill, as part of the story it wanted to tell about itself that it was originally in tension with the larger world around the issues of racial inclusion, having defined itself as part of the radical promiscuous rabble constituting the monstrous hydra—this story, with all its complications, makes Terrill's scripture-inflected revisionism all the more insidious and violent. In the slightly later period in which Terrill writes, the church defines its constituency and its ideology as white and, as such, at the expense of, albeit in sentimental memory of, Francis the "Ethyopian." She is after all rendered silent to us. We can only speculate about how Francis used scriptures, how she declaimed scripturally during and beyond the gatherings and what she would have made of the scriptural passages Terrill played with.[35] How might she have scripturalized her existence, her humanness?

On the other side of Terrill's scripturalization Bunyan's runaway allegorical games do not seem any less violent. They do not represent simply the historical facts or the simple truth. They both reflect and create realities. His writings were, like so many other discursive (religious or otherwise) writings, viewed broadly, within and beyond European cultures, as dazzling, mystifying, "magical" in their power. Blacks in the Europe of the seventeenth and eighteenth centuries were very heavily signified as different and inferior beings whose humiliation and subjugation could be understood within a developing racial classification schema and ideology such that the cultivation of "whiteness"—associated with being the most fortunate, the strongest, most robust, most intelligent, most adventurous, and so forth—could be contrasted to the blackness of the "negroes." This development led to rather difficult and challenging situations for blacks in Britain and beyond in the larger European-dominated world.[36]

Even more than Equiano's, this story of the clearly charismatic and strong personality who was called Francis speaks loudly—about white men's magic as scripturalization, in terms of (en)scripturalization, pacification as a type of politics of language and so as a kind of rhetorical violence. It is very much worth revisiting a part of Equiano's story as another window onto this phenomenon, in this case a window onto the ways in which scriptures were deployed as tools of colonial violence, ideologically inflected. In a most riveting passage from Equiano, he figures himself as a figure of colonial power, wielding the Bible as weapon against non-English colored peoples ("Indians"):

> Recollecting a passage I had read in the life of Columbus, when he was amongst the Indians in Jamaica, where, on some occasion, he frightened them, by telling them of certain events in the heavens, I had recourse to the same expedient, and it succeeded beyond my most sanguine expectations. When I had formed my determination, I went in the midst of them ... I pointed up to the heavens ... I told them God lived there, and he was angry with them ... and if they did not leave off, and go away quietly, I would take the book (pointing to the bible), read, and *tell* God to make them dead. This was something like magic. (208)

The events described in this passage took place among the "Musquito Indians" in Jamaica. Equiano relates the strange events as part of a "new adventure" that he signed on for at the request of the "celebrated"[37] Dr. Irving. Having purchased a 150-ton sloop, Dr. Irving wanted Equiano to join him in the adventure that involved setting up a slave plantation in Jamaica. Equiano indicates that, after some conversation with friends, he accepted the offer, with the commitment to use the time as opportunity, oddly enough, to advance his missionary work: "knowing that the harvest was fully ripe in those parts ... I hope to be an instrument, under God ... bringing some poor sinner to ... Jesus Christ" (202).

Even before embarking on the trip he was able to turn to his stated interest and set the tone for the narration of the adventure: He began to evangelize four "Indians" he met through Dr. Irving. Among them was the son of the king of the Musquitos. The scion and his companions had been in England for twelve months, having been involved in complex economic and political schemes with traders "for some selfish ends" (202).[38] The prince had been baptized and given the name George and taught "pretty good English," but, according to Equiano, had not been sufficiently catechized. So on the way to Jamaica Equiano set out to teach the prince English letters and basic British-inflected protestant ideology ("doctrines of Christianity"), complete with one of the books that next to the Bible was in protestant England of the time most cherished, *Fox's Martyrology*.[39]

Equiano's catechetical-propaganda program seemed to work fairly well—until the "poor heathen" was taunted by ship crewmembers as being among "true sons of Belial." This reflected doubt about the prince's training and newfound Christian piety. This taunting caused the prince to go into retreat, refusing to "learn his book" or associate with the crewmembers. Confused about the situation in which white sailors were taunting him for engaging white ways taught him by a black man, he directed to Equiano the question that I think Equiano the writer assumes the (mostly white) readers no doubt had in mind about Equiano the writer in general terms: "How comes it that all the white men on board, who can read and write, observe the sun, and know all things, yet swear, lie, and get drunk, only excepting yourself?" (204).

The answer given by the narrativized Equiano—"they do not fear God"—reflects conventional British evangelical piety and as such is Equiano the writer's answer to the question raised. Equiano the writer has with the raised question already made the much more important issue—the association of whiteness with Christian piety and doctrine and with English reading and writing, and its puzzling representation by a black man. The puzzlement and counterintuitiveness or paradox that this representation causes is voiced, from the perspective of and in the terminology created by white dominants, an "Indian," an *other* Other. Of course, what Equiano has done with this incident is to shock readers into rethinking what face is or can be associated with English-inflected Christian doctrine and piety. Can a black face represent such? It is through the unwitting but disturbing testimony of the "heathen" "Indian" other as well as the white crewmembers that Equiano's black face is in Equiano's story declared representative of Christian piety. English reading and writing continue to be associated in the minds of all with white persons, but Equiano's rendering of this incident was intended to shock and destabilize such assumptions and force defamiliarization and reconsideration to the point that the tribal representation of Christianity is scrambled and thrown into confusion.

But Equiano was not done. He proceeded as writer to do more to represent himself as a transgressive figure who causes double takes and confusion. He depicted himself with Dr. Irving reaching Jamaica and being very much involved in the purchasing of human beings— as slaves!—for the establishment of a plantation. He makes the point that he chose as slaves "all of my own countrymen, some of whom came from Lybia" (205). Most important here is the shocking fact of Equiano's involvement in slave-trafficking of black peoples, even as he registers his identification with them as a person of African descent. He presents himself as a black Christian evangelical with missionizing commitments who also facilitates the purchasing of black peoples as slaves for a white-owned plantation system! The young Musquito ("Indian") prince was right to raise the question—Who is the white man here?! No wonder the prince was confused. He spoke for many readers—the world seemed upside down: the black stranger assumed the prerogatives, the strange speech and practices and piety, of white men.

But such bizarre incidents seemed only to be a narratological setup for the most dramatic and poignant depiction of Equiano as a white man. The narration continues: Having sailed from Jamaica to a place called Cape Gracias a Dios on the Musquito shore,[40] Equiano and his company greeted and engaged natives on what seems like the usual terms of first contact between Europeans and Others, with the usual white men's perspectives and sensibilities—"we used them well." Cargo goods, alcohol among them, were offered for exchange. The natives offered to help clear the land for the planned plantation (205).

Equiano's consciousness and orientation are clearly registered as having been determined by that of white protestant evangelicalism.[41] The most dramatic and disturbing registration of the state of such consciousness is to be done in connection with the use of scriptures, more specifically in terms of the refraction of (British-inflected) mimetics of scripturalization. Feeling safe, Equiano and his company set up camp among the peoples of the honest and amiable "nation." The company had heard about but not yet encountered the great and powerful man who was the "Indian governor." The latter, we are told, traveled in high style among the peoples in different districts and provinces in order to hear and settle differences. Having heard about the encampment of Equiano's company, the governor sent notice ahead—with a stick as sign—about his intention to visit. In response, Equiano's company sent him some of the usual items of first-contact-era cargo—rum, sugar, gunpowder. In the flesh, the governor was, according to Equiano, not at all "a grave reverend judge, solid and sagacious," but instead loud and rather crude. He was full of the liquor that Equiano and his company had supplied. As such, he seemed already to have been manipulated by and was in part a caricatured creation of the white world Equiano represented. In terms narratological and political the governor was being set up for what was to come.

It was when the drunken governor struck and took the hat of one of the local native chiefs that things really got out of hand. Chaos and confusion ensued. Dr. Irving made what seemed to Equiano a feeble attempt to calm things down. He proved to be unsuccessful and out of frustration and panic he escaped into the woods. As Equiano tells the rest of the story, he was left to exercise leadership and come up with a "stratagem"[42] (208) to deal with the situation. The reader is then led to the comments that were quoted above in which Equiano recollects a passage from his reading about Columbus's adventure with "Indians in Jamaica."[43]

The specific incident to which Equiano alludes took place during Columbus's fourth voyage. The incident does not seem to have
been recounted by Columbus; it was, like so many stories about his
experiences and exploits, recorded and embellished by admirers and
tradents. Among these were Diego Méndez de Segura, who sailed on
the fourth voyage with Columbus and is described as majordomo and
arch-defender of Columbus and traditions around him;[44] Ferdinand
Columbus,[45] the second son of Columbus, a learned man who wrote
a biography of his father; and Bartolomé de las Casas, a Spanish
Dominican priest who wrote a history of the part of the world that
Columbus "discovered," including the havoc it wrought.[46]

According to Mendez and Ferdinand, the general situation that is
the backdrop to the incident is as follows. Columbus and his party
found themselves in Jamaica shipwrecked without food and supplies.
Columbus dispatched a small company to go to Hispaniola for help.
Through bartering and flattery, trickery and deceit, bullying and
intimidation, Columbus and his crew ingratiated themselves to and
manipulated the natives. For a long period they depended upon the
natives for food. But the trickery and manipulation and rewards of the
exchange system wore thin. So according to Mendez:

> the Indians became disaffected and would not bring food as before.
> [Columbus] caused all the caciques [native leaders] to be summoned and
> told them they he marveled that they should not bring food as they had
> been accustomed to do, knowing that, as he had told them, he had come
> there by the command of God and that God was offended with them
> and that on that very night He would show this to them by signs which
> He would cause to appear in the heavens. And as on that night there
> was an almost total eclipse of the moon, he told them that God did this
> from anger with them because they did not bring food. They believed
> him and were very terrified, and they promised that they would always
> bring him food .[47]

In terms of the sensibilities that characterized his world, Mendez
seemed to have exercised some restraint in the recording of the

incident: He held back from taunting or registering contempt for what from his world perspective was the ignorance and weaknesses of the natives. Instead, he focused on the resolve and courage of Columbus.

Ferdinand Columbus added a few more and different details, sensibilities and perspectives, especially regarding the factor of belief in God—the ample amount displayed by his father (and also obviously held by him), the utter lack of it displayed by the natives. For Ferdinand such belief meant power. His father, he judged, possessed a great amount of it, and the natives registered only fear and incredulity:

As for the Indians, God was very angry with them for neglecting to bring us food for which we paid them by barter, and had determined to punish them with famine and pestilence. To convince the incredulous, God would send them a clear token from Heaven of the punishment they were about to receive. They should therefore attend that night the rising of the moon: She would rise inflamed with wrath, signifying the chastisement God would visit upon them ...

... at the rising of the moon the eclipse began, and the higher it rose the more complete the eclipse became, at which the Indians grew so frightened that with great howling and lamentation they came running from all directions to the ships, laden with provisions, and praying the Admiral to intercede with God that He might not vent His wrath upon them, and promising they would diligently supply all their needs in the future. The Admiral replied that he wished to speak briefly with his God, and retired to his cabin while the eclipse waxed and the Indians cried all the time for his help. When the Admiral perceived that the crescent phase of the moon was finished and that it would soon shine forth clearly, he issued from his cabin, saying that he had appealed to his God and prayed for them and had promised Him in their name that henceforth they would be good and treat the Christians well, bringing provisions and all else they needed ... Perceiving that what he said was coming true, they offered many thanks to the Admiral and uttered praises of his God as long as the eclipse continued. From that time forward they were diligent in providing us with all we needed, and were loud in praise of the Christian God. For they believed that eclipses were

91

very harmful, and since they were ignorant of their cause and of their regular recurrence and did not suspect that men living on earth could know what was happening in the sky, they were certain that his God had revealed that eclipse to the Admiral.[48]

What is important to Equiano in referencing the incident from "Columbus" (the Columbus tradition) clearly has to do with the dominant power of the world of white folks. In this instance the dominance was reflected in the "signs" or "tokens"—part of a system of their world's "magic." The magic entailed control of the heavens, including the moon. Columbus is understood to be in direct communication with a powerful god who controls the heavens. Communication with the gods produced a kind of knowing that was a form of power that could be called upon and demonstrated anywhere and seemingly for any purpose.

It is not likely that the incident was ever intended to represent anything other than the display of the dominance of the white men and their world represented by Columbus. This dominance seemed to turn not in this instance around the expected or traditional weapons of war, but around a special item of cargo, knowledge—secret knowledge of the ways and will of the gods. Columbus is depicted as knowing things, things that the others, the "savages," did not and could not know. It is this special knowledge about the gods that the natives are depicted as reacting to with awe and terror, reacting to it as some kind of magic, something without explanation or containment.

Of course, the phenomenon that was the backdrop to this incident was the threat that the natives represented. The latter were vis-à-vis Columbus and his crews in the real position of power; they held all the cards. They were on their home turf, with all the advantages that being at home usually means. Columbus and his party were the intruders, without the means to overwhelm the natives in the usual terms of power. So in this situation the white men especially needed a trick or "stratagem" whereby the natives could be made to misrecognize their own powerful position and be rendered somewhat befuddled by the claims and wizardry of the white men. In short, in order for Columbus and his crews to survive the situation, the natives had to be made to misperceive the power situation; they had to be tricked into believing they were not powerful but ignorant and weak. Here the mechanics of power were clearly discursive and ideological. Is this not really the baseline for the experience and maintenance of power?[49]

It is clear on what basis Equiano recalled and made use of the incident involving Columbus. His experience with the Musquito natives involved precisely the same sort of power dynamics that were reflected in the stories about Columbus. Like Columbus, Equiano was away from his home turf. The "Indians" were in a commanding position and some of them, full of the confidence that meeting strangers on home turf may inspire—and no doubt full of the alcohol as cargo supplied by Equiano's party—appeared to be threatening. Also like Columbus, in order to address the situation faced, Equiano thought of a "stratagem." This term (or its equivalent), actually found in at least one account about Columbus and in Equiano's story, reflects Equiano's reading of Columbus's experience as revelation, even celebration, of Columbus's subterfuge and connivance. (It is also Equiano's recognition of his need to imitate the legendary admiral and explorer.) The point in both or all traduced situations/contexts—Equiano's narrative, the mythic accounts about Columbus, and the larger situation of contact between Europeans and the "savage" Other—was to figure out how to manipulate the natives and destabilize their positions of power. The fear of the Other led to manipulation and management.

In the incident with the Musquito natives Equiano not only invoked but identified himself as Columbus, the historical legendary figure who discovered and conquered the worlds of the "heathen." In his engagement with native "Indians"—other peoples of color—Equiano identified with the white man. This identification is rather complicated: Equiano does not mean by it that he is self-loathing and wishes to be some type of human being—white—other than what he is. He does not mean by it that he has fear and contempt for the "Indians" with whom he makes contact. And it does not mean that his perspective on the world has been hijacked or manipulated by white dominance. Of course, these claims may have been true; it is hard to tell. Arguing such would be too straightforward and too easy. All readers will have learned Equiano is far too clever as writer and that more is usually at issue than the simplest point. The "stratagem" referenced in the context of the story told about Equiano's exploits with the Musquito natives is layered and complex; it requires reading that matches the cleverness of Equiano's composition. Equiano seems to want readers to compare him to Columbus, but only insofar as he demonstrates and wields the kind of power and authority that is associated with being white. The type of power at issue in this case is knowledge, or, more broadly and poignantly, a power play that is reflective of, presumes, and draws on a larger structure of hegemony that is ideological and social-psychological in nature.

Insofar as Columbus is depicted as someone in communication with the god who controls the heavens, he is seen as powerful. His power is understood to lie not in any object but in the knowing itself or rather the capacity to communicate with God and so to know God's way. Equiano seems to recognize as much as he depicts himself as man of power in relationship to the Musquito natives. He understands his power over the natives to lie in his capacity and authority to communicate. Communication here means not merely passing along basic information, but being able and authorized to speak to God and being able to communicate what God says. And as the narrativized Equiano has already discovered (in the non-talking book story of Chapter 3 of his story), according to the assumptions of British protestant evangelicals, God talks now mainly through the book—the Bible—as the most important mode and symbol of power: "I would take the book ... the bible ... read, and tell God" (208).

In this claim to power there is the assumption that the natives are ignorant and credulous, easily frightened and manipulable. It is all the more fascinating to note that Equiano used the same descriptors as he told readers about incidents and adventures in earlier moment of his life. He described himself as being, before enlightenment, almost always terrified and shocked by and naïve in the ways of the white world.[50] And the people he claimed as his own people, the Igbos, were described in his chapter one as being prone to believe things that were incredible and superstitious. They were described as being under the sway of magicians and wise men. Surely, the point was to make description of the Musquitos recall the description of the Igbos and to make the reader understand the two peoples as those who are not enlightened by (protestant evangelical) truths.

Given Equiano's comparison—his "strong analogy"—of the Igbos to the (ancient-biblical world) Jews, his speculation whether "the one people had sprung from the other," no doubt in imitation of modern-world European Christians' penchant for comparing themselves as such,[51] Equiano must have considered all peoples—including all groups of Europeans—to be subject to the magicians and wise men of their respective worlds and forms of magic. In light of such a "strong analogy," should we not wonder whether the ancient Jews were not in Equiano's mind also subject to such forces? "Like the Israelites in their primitive state, our government was conducted by our chiefs, our judges, our wise men and elders" (44).

Now if most peoples—including Jews and Europeans—are subject to magicians and wise men and their magic, surely so the "heathen." In other words, Equiano seems to have projected from his own thinking about and experiences of British culture some things about Igbo and Musquito culture. His and Columbus's engagements with and manipulations of the heathenish other were based on their own experiences and observances of and assumptions about such phenomena. There certainly had been and remained European folk traditions that were characterized as "magic" of various forms.[52] But even more to the point for Equiano, with his rather special if not unique positionality as black stranger who belied so many of his experiences and adventures, the dominant arrangements and relations of power in Britain and throughout Europe that had come to disdain the folk traditions and their orientations to "magic" nonetheless could be thought about in terms of "magic." These dominant arrangements and relations of power, after all, included evangelical Christianity and its orientation to biblical interpretation.

It would appear, then, that Equiano read and used (stories about) Columbus to think with, and to imitate. The perdurance of the incident in the memories and constructed stories about Columbus suggests its poignancy, that it captures a truth, a truth about how the dominant European world is constructed. And, of course, Equiano as the (black) stranger disturbingly positions himself—through his writing, no less—to remind readers of such truth and to make use of such a truth in order to destabilize his (bottom link on the chain of being) position as well as the larger general situation. He was not so much trying to be white as he was demonstrating how power worked in the dominant world of the Europeans. He was doing nothing if not imitating and signifying on such systems and arrangements. I assume that Equiano, like "Columbus," assumed that certain tricks that work at home, among the *hoi polloi* and even those above them, might—with some modifications—work abroad among savages and heathens. Their manipulations rested upon crude but clever assumptions about societies and cultures, about social psychology across cultures. In imitating "Columbus," Equiano was showing that he knew how power as understood by the Europeans could be worked. He depicted himself not so much as a white man for the general sake of assuming another identity but as a man using power.

What begs further consideration is the type of power or magic that Equiano depicts himself displaying. Two observations are first in order: Whatever else may be at issue, the power that Equiano imitates and wields is ideological and social-psychological, and it is extensive—it extends beyond the borders of the homeland nation of the wielder of power.

Of course, Equiano does not use the term "power"; he uses instead the term "magic" in order to convey what is at work.[53] The one concept stands in for the other. "Magic" may simply be used to capture the essence or nature of operations of something that is confusing or puzzling. That power aptly names what is at stake for Equiano is clear enough through a reading of his story. His entire story is really about the quest for power that he associates with white men. He depicts himself as one whose life represents dramatic changes in terms of such power—from abject powerlessness, as a slave, to one who, as in the incident with the Musquitos, represents a European version of Christian faith and wields power in the tradition of one of the most legendary of white Christian men. So insofar as the power is white men's magic, Equiano understands his quest to be to pursue and obtain white men's magic.

This power as magic is psychologically felt and ideological in nature. There was no object or thing that in either situation was dangled before and pointed to the credulous natives as offensive weapon. All Columbus had, all that Equiano had, was a suggestion, an idea, an image. What was traded on or exploited was the very idea—shared by natives and Catholic Spanish and protestant British alike—of an anthropomorphized god who through various media and in various ways talks and listens to certain human beings. The latter are thereby rendered powerful. Their power is evident in and tied to the communication or the authority or ability to participate in and understand and translate such communication.

But such an arrangement turns around a type of suspension—of doubt regarding the truth or reality of what is faced. And it involves acceptance of certain assumptions and claims about reality. It is not a heavier burden to believe that strange-looking and strange-talking "men" who arrive on one's shores from a distance are mysterious and powerful. It is not a stretch to accept that such men are in communication with forces that are unknown and potentially threatening. And it is very understandable that a group would give respect to one among such strange men who holds forth and declares with a sense of authority in ways similar to how an indigenous magician or wise man might have. It is also unsurprising that one would give pause when such figures claim that they had spoken to and heard from a god regarding the causes of unexpected outsized events such as the darkening of the moon or regarding the explicit threat of death against one's company. This was the assumption and orientation of most human societies. What "Columbus" and "Equiano" are depicted as having done is exploit the social psychology—with its fears, insecurities, expectations, and hopes—of a particular context and time. That is what magicians do. That is their power. That is the work and effect of the Wizard of Oz.[54]

97

The phenomenon of the workings of the Wizard of Oz—magic, sleight of hand—is now understood as quite common, especially in the fraught contexts and time periods of first contact, extending from the fifteenth to the nineteenth century. The experiences of contact between the West and the Rest, between Europeans as travelers/explorers/merchants/conquerors and the "discovered" savages/heathen as the Other represented a kind of stage that inspired the production and performance of types of what Equiano discovers as white men's magic.[55] It was in the contact zones that difference was discovered, interpreted, and negotiated, or out of a sense of fear or threat covered up or undermined or exploited.

Focusing on the past two hundred years or so of contact zone experiences and responses in her fascinating book that is an anthology of indigenous peoples' stories about "white men," Julia Blackburn's *The White Men: The First Response of Aboriginal Peoples to the White Man* (1979),[56] provides perspective on what may have been at work in Equiano's storytelling. Told by those who encounter strange intruders from unknown places, the stories in Blackburn's book establish some aspects of the social psychology, the anxieties and fears and hopes that condition the responses, perspectives, and sentiments that have been noted among aboriginal peoples in such situations:

> It is as if creatures from outer space were to land in one of our cities. The news of their arrival travels at a desperate speed from place to place, from country to country. The simple facts of the situation become immediately confused with the private fears and imaginings of each individual who hears what has happened, and soon many wild and contradictory stories are in circulation.
>
> There would be those who believe that the arrival of the white men must be a sign presaging the end of a troubled world, and they then realize that they have been expecting such an event for a long time. Others would perhaps trust that these are benevolent intruders who have been sent to help the human race and bring a new golden age into being. One person becomes hysterical and the mood infects a whole group, because this is a time of mass responses. Even if these strange creatures travel

about very little and do no harm to their hosts, just the knowledge of their existence forces people to reassess completely their sense of their own place within the universe ... (26)

Among the responses she records in the book is one that involves the devolution of power of the kings of the Ambo in the region in Africa in what is present-day Namibia and Angola. After the 1861 ritual murder of Haimibili, the greatest of the Ambo kings, each successive ruler became less and less powerful until the last king, Mandume, was killed in 1917. What followed was a succession of local and regional headmen who over time came to be ruled by white colonial government officials. In response to this situation the prophet Muselanga included prophecies in a layered poem written over a period of about twenty years—from the 1870s to the 1890s:

> Something strange is creeping over the waters;
> Foreigners creep in to the country.
> It was far, it comes near, it is here.
> People start to walk.
> Perhaps an omuhama tree will fall across their path.
> The strange people come from a distant country,
> They come with different words.
> When they are talking they should be listened to.
>
> I walked and walked through the country
> And I saw the kraals of the nobles.
> I walked a second time through the country
> I did not see the kraals of the nobles
> But white men's houses I have seen.
>
> Oejulu! I do not see the kraal of the King.
> I do not see the kraals of the nobles.
> Only the kraal of the woman Naminda I see.
> White men's houses I see in what were the fields of
>   Haindongo.

Houses I see like white millet meal.
The world will end, it will end completely.
The King will die, he will go underground to the palace
    of the frog.
I will go away from here, I will go underground into the
    hole of the bees.
I will go in a clothing of earth
For I have cursed the King.
  (38–39)

The point to be taken from such prophecy is that the coming and continuing presence of white men brought chaos and anxiety. The strange thing is also the problematic and fearful thing. The continuing presence of white men provides an opportunity to reflect on and to project in expressive forms what accounts for their strangeness. An early-twentieth-century Kongolese wooden statue[57] of a white man with his dog alongside him provides an example of what is seen and what is found fascinating and curious. The not-so-striking but altogether plain figure of the white man wears a hat that looks much like that belonging to some sort of (civilian) official, and full-length semi-official uniformed clothing. And he is bedecked with all sorts of things—things that look like jewelry, religious emblems, utensils, weapons. In other words, white men's stuff. It is speculated that the figure carries a variety of magical emblems used as part of a healing cult. It is hard not to suppose that the assumption was that the white men possessed and had access to many sorts of symbols and media of magical powers.

A more striking representation can be seen in a colorful scene (Figure 2.2) painted onto the henta boards from the Nicobar Islands, located southeast of the Indian subcontinent.[58] A white man is depicted as a ship's captain who juggles and is otherwise surrounded by many objects, goods of cargo, including an umbrella, a pipe, a compass, a telescope, a light, a clock, some furniture. With so many objects that put so many things in motion to such powerful effects at his command, the white man is considered to be the embodiment of God.

Figure 2.2 A "henta-koi" that acted as a magical charm. It is painted with an image of a white man who appears to be dressed in the jacket of a sea captain. He is surrounded by the numerous symbols of European omnipotence: mirrors, clocks, umbrella, knives, etc. Cargo cult. Nicobar Islands, India. Late 19th–early 20th CE. Painted wood. British Museum. Photo credit: Werner Forman/Art Resource, NY.

What do these images suggest? It is apparent and understandable that in the contact zone, in confrontation with the sudden and dramatic appearance of strangers in their midst, indigenous peoples register understandable anxiety and fear and a sense of being challenged, threatened, even overwhelmed. Showing up from distant lands—and with "cargo," no less—is itself a display of power. It makes sense that the speech—the proclamations and threats—of the white-faced strangers under the dramatic circumstances of first contact would be taken seriously and warily. The larger point to make here, in sum, is that these strangers appeared powerful on account of their strange tricks, including their various media of communication and representation.

I think it is clear that "Equiano" (the simple character in the contained little story; the writerly Equiano who is a more complex figure will provoke below another interpretation) and "Columbus" (the legendary, not the historical, figure), representing "white men" in the contact zone, did not care, perhaps were not self-aware enough, to reveal the truth about the layered thinking and capacities of such people. They preferred their indigenous peoples to be remembered as simple, flat, ignorant, credulous, superstitious. This is the prejudiced view—the scripturalization—of such peoples that we, as equally flat and prejudiced modern and contemporary readers, are provided and have unfortunately mostly accepted and maintained.

Now, regarding the "white men," their part of the modern agenda of nation creep, of conquering other lands and extending national dominance, needs to be acknowledged. Equiano seemed to have understood the agenda this way. So it seems the success of reaching, if not always the planned place, certainly a very different and faraway place, inspired a mixture of arrogance and fear and an assumption about superior power and fear and trepidation. This was a volatile mixture, to be sure. As the competition in all arenas—military, political, economic, cultural/religious—continued unabated among nations of early modern Europe, it extended into exploration and expropriation of other lands. And that such interest led often to trickery and manipulation in addition to violence few would deny.

What concerns me most about this phenomenon are the efforts on the part of the "white men" to project and communicate superiority and cover up their fear and anxiety. There are many examples from contact zones that show how pacification—precisely of the type that the DC in Achebe's *TFA* thought about—is attempted and achieved through the violence that is (en)scripturalization, the inscription of the indigenous into the colonial scriptural economy.

When the reader comes to the final part of the chapter of *TFA* there is no doubt that the impact of the DC and the world regime he represents in Umuofia is critical—in fact, "catastrophic" is not too strong a descriptor. The shock. The resignation. The suicide. The silence. The trembling. The choked words. The dispersion. The despair. No one is speaking. That is what scripturalization does—it renders one silent, mute, or a stutterer (when it is not facilitating death, social and otherwise). There is no getting beyond it. Like the sentiments of the Negro spiritual, it's too high—you cannot get over it; too low—cannot get under it; too wide—cannot get around it. You have to go in through the door. Scripturalization, indeed. Slavery, indeed.

Might "things fall apart" actually be judged to be too much an exercise in (British-influenced) euphemy? Notwithstanding the economy of Achebe's words at the end—or perhaps as a profound reflection of the situation—the effects of British pacification on Umuofia are profound and long-lasting. Anyone who doubts the efficacy and ongoing effects of scripturalization should take note of the social-cultural and religious orientations, what some might call religious fundamentalisms— with their political-economic ramifications—of modern-day formerly colonized countries of sub-Saharan Africa, the Caribbean, parts of the Americas and Asia.[59]

One rather dramatic example is enough here—that having to do with contempt for and proscriptions and statutes and sanctioned violence against homosexuals and same-sex marriages and related issues (such as ordination, adoption). Our headlines indicate that such positions are defended by the formerly colonized/formerly enslaved—in Kenya, Nigeria, and beyond in Africa, and in much of African America in the United States—in the name of the authority of colonial-world-invented and—"donated" scriptures.

In many such situations in the twenty-first century the strongest, even if not the only, line of influence is clear and obvious: The colonial missionizing presence and influence are even today very much intact in some places.[60] The gain of political independence notwithstanding, the donation of the colonial that is pacification that is also scripturalization ensures that things, having fallen apart, sadly remain so.

That is, until mimetic (scripturalizing) practices begin to be taken up and reconsidered and reexamined in critical historical terms. These practices reconsidered and redeployed represent tracks laid for a possibly different history—of sensibilities, orientations, self-understandings, power relations, formations. They are the focus of the next chapter.

CHAPTER 3

"WE HAVE FALLEN APART"

THE RUPTURE OF MEANING

> Umuofia was like a startled animal with ears erect,
> sniffing the silent, ominous air,
> and not knowing which way to run.
>
> —*Things Fall Apart, Chapter 23*

"We have fallen apart." This jolting sentiment is articulated several times, in different ways, through different characters, and on different levels of consciousness and meaning in *TFA*. Not only do Okonkwo and Obierika openly express the sentiment with these and in other words within the narrative, but through the title and the twists and end of the drama the narrator also shows himself to be very much in line with the sentiment. There are different meanings in the carriers of the sentiment within the narrative.

Okonkwo, as a tragic figure around whom so much of the drama turns, not only expresses the truth about what has happened but also embodies it. Insofar as he represents the traditional (but ratcheted up) masculinist or aggressive figure, narcissistic, full of hubris, lacking in sensitivity, easily rattled and prone to violent outbursts, hypersensitive to slights and to change, he is in these respects made to be a high-profile figure of Umuofia who, too long in denial about the turn things have taken, the changes in the world about him, fitfully and tragically comes to the point of falling apart by hanging himself.

Obierika is also a representative figure. He is ever-observant, respectful but ever-questioning of the way things are traditionally done in the village. He recognizes early on the profound changes taking place around him in the village, and he seemingly, even if warily, opens himself to a future and what he and others may make of it, paradoxically apparently open to building on the experience of falling apart and surviving thereby.

As the narrator/writer, Achebe clearly seems to identify much more with Obierika insofar as Okonkwo is a tragic figure and Obierika is characterized strongly and in a positive light. But beyond this identification, Achebe signals the similar more expanded messages he wants to convey in the books that would follow *TFA*, books that as messages of critique and hope use the experience of things having fallen apart as springboard. There is no doubt through which character Achebe speaks.

The import of the message conveyed or stance taken by Obierika in response to the calamity faced by Umuofia can more sharply be seen in relationship to at least two other responses. These two responses in relationship to Obierika's/Achebe's response constitute something of a complex dialectics of orientation in Umuofia, with corresponding fates. They can in my view be correlated with the emphases that are fleshed out in Achebe's other novels. These other works can be lined up in chronological and in narratological terms in relationship to *TFA*.[1]

I categorize these three Umuofian responses as (1) assimilation/simple mimetics, (2) resistance/implosion/rigid mimetics, and (3) psycho-social-cultural marronage/mimetic excess.

Assimilation or simple mimetics is the way I characterize the first response. This characterization is intended to capture the response to the intrusion of the white people into the world—the rhythms and practices—of the Umuofia village. Achebe makes it clear that this intrusion—invasion, actually—represents the falling apart of Umuofia as white domination in the form of the imposition of colonial government and all that pertains to it. And poignantly he indicates that nothing more dramatically reflects the falling apart than "conversion"—the strange and puzzling turn to the white man's absurd "religion"—on the part of many in the clan. This turn is presented on what I think are the refreshingly accurate critical-analytical terms that help the reader understand that the white men's "religion"—modeled and translated most powerfully and intensely by the missionaries—is a fundamental part, if not in fact the critical core and chief instrument, of their "government." After being converted, little more according to the narrative needed to be done to or with a member of the clan to secure his or her loyalty to the new regime. The rhetorics on the part of both groups seemed to suggest that the resocialization was thick, absolute; converts seemed to consider themselves more or less outside the clan, and were for the most part considered by the members of the clan to be outside the clan.

Within the clan, white men's religion had been generally considered "lunatic" (*TFA*, 101). Although the narrator indicates and has a few characters concede that there were some quite legitimate and compelling reasons for turning to the white men's world—including, for example, being labeled impure or of low and outsider caste status by the clan; and the claim among the Christians that all, irrespective of frailties, weaknesses, and so forth, are brothers and sisters of equal status—the turn was nonetheless considered by observers inside the village as something shocking, even destructive. Okonkwo never failed to express his contempt for and anger about the phenomenon. That his son Nyowe became a convert was simply too much for him to bear. Words hardly served to express his rage. The situation was a reflection on him, on his status in the clan.

This response that was the turn to the white men's religion can be seen from within or close up as an actual range of social-cultural orientations and representations—from zealotry or fanaticism to the mildest inflection. These internal differences in representations notwithstanding, I think it appropriate to categorize the phenomenon in terms of what I call simple mimetics, but mimetics that represent radical change, a fundamental change in orientation, in outlook on the world or reality. This change represents acceptance and assimilation of the ways of the white men and the rejection of traditional ways. A sharp absolutist contrast between the two ways and worlds is accepted.

Nyowe may be considered representative here insofar as he rather provocatively and shockingly indicated that as "one of them" Okonkwo was no longer to be considered his father (83). He had been "capti-vated" by the religion's "poetry," "felt in the marrow." He was moved by the fervor and passion felt through song and by the Christian circle's compassion for those thrown aside by the clan. These characteristics puzzled him; they were also compelling enough to get him to turn (85).

Now to Enoch, who is another example of simple mimetics. He was something else: His response was to go all out to show himself to be an earnest and authentic convert, taking seriously the missionaries' proclamation that "There is only one true God." Considered one of the "over-zealous converts" whose zeal had been held in check by one of the moderate missionaries from an earlier time, he "flourished in full flavor." So zealous was he that he was known as "the outsider who wept louder than the bereaved." Elaborate description by the narrator was a cutting indictment and hardly masks the contempt held for him:

> Enoch was short and slight of build, and always seemed in great haste. His feet were short and broad, and when he stood or walked his heels came together and his feet opened outwards as if they had quarreled and meant to go in different directions. Such was the excessive energy bottled up in Enoch's small body that it was always erupting in great quarrels and fights. On Sundays he always imagined that the sermon was preached for the benefit of his enemies ... (105)

This tightly wound figure thought that there was no more dramatic way to demonstrate the truth of this proclamation than by doing some-thing unheard of in the village, something considered sacrilegious: the killing (that is to say, the unmasking) of one of the *egwugwu*. He did so and thereby set in motion chaos and confusion and conflict (108f). This was mimetics of the closed-circle kind, simple and tight, the sort of "binding" and "suturing" to and mirroring of the "master's culture" that smelled of social death, a "reflexive circuit of self-abjection."[2]

The second response also represents mimetics, but of a different kind from the first response. It can be thought of as a kneejerk response, a response that is on the surface or at first glance is the direct opposite of the first response. But the rigidity reflects and leads to precisely the effects rejected and denied and deemed problematic. Okonkwo is the (only) character who in focus perfectly exemplifies this category. This big man in the village, this renowned wrestler, this man who always wanted to be the best at all that counted is characterized as a ticking time bomb. His impulsiveness and his eagerness to withstand any changes—real or proposed—define him. But of course he ends up paradoxically following the "script" imagined or written for him and the clan: His reactions—the rhetorical fire, the rage, the violence (110)—are those easily imagined and anticipated by colonial officials. Insofar as he does not grow as a character, to the extent that he does not learn from situations, as he seems unable to cope with change, he becomes a caricature and an unattractive and unsympathetic figure in the eyes of all. Most significant, he makes his attitude and behavior in its opposition a direct reflection of the dynamics set in motion by the colonials. His brittleness and his volatility signal his personal insecurity as well as the belief that the traditions of the village cannot stand with strength and integrity before and against the ways of the white world. He seemed to suggest that the situation required (only) an exaggerated, overdetermined translation of tradition, a complex and hapless and ironic mimetics, to be sure.

The reader is made aware of Okonkwo as one who is ultra-authoritarian. He enjoyed having those around him, including his wives, tremble in fear of his reactions to circumstances (9). In fact, fear seemed to be the central running theme in the narrative in describing, even psychoanalyzing, him: "His whole life was dominated by fear, the fear of failure and of weakness" (10). There was also much insecurity and shame (13) and vengefulness. He was bitter, choked with hate (113, 115), much prone to anxiety, and stressed out (note the constant teeth grinding), so violent acts as the way to solve problems with all those encountered (19, 21, 38) seemed to him the only way to go.

Hypersensitive, Okonkwo was among the first to see and register concern about the changes going on in the village. "[D]eeply grieved," he was the one of the two characters in the narrative to acknowledge that Umuofia was "breaking up and falling apart" (104). However, his response—the impulsive killing of another out of hot anger and hatred and then his taking of his own life, out of despair, helplessness, and hopelessness—was the ultimate, the literal, embodied breakup and falling apart. In spite of his heroics, his passion, his courage, this response left no route, no option, no strategic defensive or offensive war plan for the village he loved so much. He was a tragic figure. There could not have been a more tragic set of events for the village.

The two responses discussed above—two related but distinguishable types of mimetics—provide a useful perspective on the response that seems to me to capture Achebe's position and that of the most sympathetic and attractive, if not most complex, character. This response is advanced not only through what Achebe has the narrator add as gloss or commentary, but also through Obierika as character. I suggest calling this response not so much the middle way but the way that complexly steers clear of the other two, as part of a dialectic of response to the crisis of seeing things falling part. This third way—Obierika's way, the postcolonial, black modernist way—involves accepting the reality and challenge of change even as he questions and challenges and confronts both old ways and new impositions.

Obierika is throughout the story clearly aware of the need to reform some ways that have defined Umuofia—the exiling of some, the killing of others, as poignant and wrenching examples. Some observances, he thought, needed to be tweaked, others needed to be discarded, and yet others were to be held onto, cherished. He seems to represent the courage to face the problems and challenges of tradition. He is also very much aware of the need to face squarely the presence and strange ways of the colonials. Perhaps, his character communicates to all, some rapprochement is possible with the strangers and some discerning, critical, and strategic way forward might be possible. Perhaps, but more needs to be learned, considered. The presence of the strangers inspires him to voice what turns out to be the chief theme of the story—things have indeed fallen apart. This is both a declaration and a complaint—a complaint against some ways of the village, a declaration that the ways of the village were being directly and indirectly undermined and overturned by the white strangers. Obierika proclaims not only that this is so, but also in what respects it is so.

On one occasion in conversation with Okonkwo, Obierika remarked about his anguish and sadness in seeing young men of the village "killing palm trees in the name of tapping"—"Sometimes I wish I had not taken the *ozo* title." When Okonkwo responded, with his characteristic rigidity—"the law of the land must be obeyed"—Obierika's characteristic sensitive and questioning mind is revealed: "I don't know how we got that law" (42). This seemingly insignificant exchange reflects Obierika's self-critical thinking and orientation and that of an important segment of the larger culture.

It was Obierika who first acknowledges that things are not as they should be in Umuofia. He put the matter first rather colorfully—the white man "has put a knife on the things that held us together and we have fallen apart" (100). This was a strong statement from one who is depicted as always questioning the ways things are done. He was known as "a man who thought about things." Often he could not find answers to his own difficult questions, but he refused to fall back into the safety of simplicity:

> Why should a man suffer so grievously for an offense he committed inadvertently? ... He remembered his wife's twin children whom he had thrown away. What crime had they committed? The Earth had decreed that they were an offence on the one land and must be destroyed. And if the clan did not exact punishment for an offence against the great goddess, her wrath was loosed on all the land and not just on the offender. As the elders said, if one finger brought oil it soiled the others. (74)

He demonstrated his wisdom, his expansive thinking, and his fair-mindedness in his willingness both to talk to enemies and to level criticism against different sides of issues. He was actually willing to negotiate with and challenge the DC and his representatives. He was also willing to defend and to challenge fellow Umuofians (116f).

Obierika's description and analysis of Okonkwo's death and what it represented and portended is important. He is said to have spoken directly and "ferociously" to the DC the following words: "That man was one of the greatest men in Umuofia. You drove him to kill himself; and now he will be buried like a dog" (117).

These were his final words in the novel; he uttered them as he trembled and choked. The words provoked an almost violent response from one of the DC's men, but nothing from the DC himself—at least not in direct response. It is worth noting here that Obierika's sentiment comes close to—I think, is one and the same with—the narrator's/ Achebe's powerful and poignant richly textured summary description of the larger tense situation, included at an earlier moment, on the night of the arrest of the representative six men of the village who had been called to appear before the DC to answer for the burning of the Christian church:

> This story spread quickly through the villages, and was added to as it went. Some said that the men had already been taken to Umuru and would be hanged on the following day. Some said that their families would also be hanged. Others said that soldiers were already on their way to shoot the people of Umuofia as they had done in Abame.
>
> It was the time of the full moon. But that night the voice of children was not heard. The village *ilo* where they always gathered for a moon-play was empty. The women of Iguedo did not meet in their secret enclosure to learn a new dance to be displayed later to the village. Young men who were always abroad in the moonlight kept their huts that night. Their manly voices were not heard on the village paths as they went to visit their friends and lovers. *Umuofia was like a startled animal with ears erect, sniffing the silent, ominous air and not knowing which way to turn.* (111, my emphasis)

This response on the part of the village—otherwise paradoxically summarized as "silence"—reflects awareness of something having gone terribly wrong, of things having deteriorated, spun out of control. It is a summation that reflects Obierika's/Achebe's view not only of the devolution and deterioration of the situation, but the corresponding terms and order of a future beyond it.

Obierika's response to the challenges around him suggests wide and profound implications for critical analysis—of modern postcolonial and post-enslaved Africa and African diasporas. In one respect Achebe, with his other novels that followed *TFA* as realistic historical fiction—*No Longer a Ease* (1960), *Arrow of God* (1964), *A Man of the People* (1966), *Anthills of the Savannah* (1987), among the most important—took up just such an analysis. The judgments of critics about the literary merits of such works aside, I find fascinating and intriguing Achebe's efforts in these works to chart (and encourage and critique) the course or fate of the Umuofians (and what they represent) as they undergo from the late nineteenth century into the mid-twentieth century significant and wrenching changes. These changes represent the experiences of many tribes and villages, especially the humiliating loss of their independence and traditions and control of their lands. They find themselves roiling and twisting, with setbacks and more humiliations as they go through the pangs of regaining their independence and becoming no more a village in simple terms but part of a modern nation. With these novels Achebe as artist opens wide and provocative windows onto the struggles on the part of humiliated peoples—postcolonial west Africa—to survive and find their bearings and orientation in a radically changed and challenging world. Within this genre and given his orientation to the genre, he provides less description and political prescription than social texture—precisely what I find most helpful as springboard for my analysis in this book.

Most interesting for me is the use of the motif of *things falling apart* not only in *TFA,* but also throughout the other novels. This motif—and its varied permutations in terms of labels, articulations, and ramifying behaviors—I find to be the central or defining theme of Achebe's body of fiction. What this theme suggests is that Achebe understood Obierika's proclamation to be basic truth—truth about the unstable, uneasy, challenging, and near-tragic situation in which the people about whom he writes found themselves. What we have here is acceptance of the tragic, of fallen-ness, of humiliation, as a basis for the collective self-understanding and orientation going forward in the modern world, what was then for Achebe and his contemporaries in the mid-twentieth century a heady period in terms of African political independence, conscientization, solidarity, and eventual spiral into chaos and deterioration.

This theme suggests much about how the people around whom things have fallen apart are to be interpreted, including how they themselves interpret the world. "Things fall apart" is, after all, for Achebe, British ironic understatement or euphemy[3] of a sort for the colonial regime and its forms of violence. Included in such a theme in terms of Achebe's use of it are tragedies, interruptions, and disruptions, the full nature and implications and ramifications of which have even to this day hardly been explored. Might such tragic situations and developments be understood to be consequent to or parallel with the trans-Atlantic slave trade and slavery throughout the Americas? It would seem that one possible implication of Achebe's poignant and pointed realistic historical fiction is more clearly and strongly relating (sub-Saharan or black) colonized/postcolonial "Africans" to the worldwide enslaved/post-slavery "African" diaspora. Things fallen apart used as a trope and wedge for the analysis of such peoples is quite promising. The analysis might turn less around similar pigmentation or shared geographical and tribal origins or ethnicity in ultimate terms, and much more profoundly around experience—the experience of things having falling apart on the terms registered in the novels. Such experience totally reframes, even if it does not delegitimize or render questionable, the old debates (think Frazier–Herskovitz) about the relationship between black Africa and the black diaspora in terms of retention (or loss) of African traditions. A focus on humiliations of the sort that have to do with what capture and enslavement and being stolen from one's homeland represent, on the one hand, and on the other, what the colonization of one's homeland represents can lead to a different conversation, rapprochement, and relationship.[4]

Thinking and strategizing and analyzing existence through or on the basis of humiliations that the imposition of the colonial order and slavery represent rather than around them or in denial of them is the

way to understand Achebe's work—at least, I should like to empha-
size, how Achebe's work might be read and made to be resonant and
compelling. Again, "things fall apart" is the pointed and freighted
abbreviated euphemy for this mindset and orientation. It may help
construct a psycho-social-political bridge built across the Atlantic
by which African and African diaspora communities see and understand one another in terms of the shared experiences of humiliations
of black peoples in the modern world. It is also suggestive of a way to
read much of the literature and arts from the mid-twentieth century in
Africa and going back to the beginning of expressiveness in the black
diaspora. *TFA* is significant as a form of such expressiveness, as it
were, paradoxically, from Africa, representing already a new African
mind, already necessarily—on account of the colonial experience—
complexly miscegenated. The title and narrative provide a provocative
and useful handle for reconsideration of historical and social analysis. The title named the condition, the situation at mid-century—on
both sides of the Atlantic, differences notwithstanding—that had to
be faced.

This new miscegenated African mind, with its honest recognition
and use of the reality of things falling apart as touchstone, is evident in
the judgment about and attitude to the world provoked by the humiliations and pulverizations of identities and traditions and worldviews
among black peoples in Africa and across the Americas.[5] There was
keen awareness among African and African diaspora peoples who
had been enslaved and colonized that much had fallen apart—so
much violence, so much loss, so much displacement, so much death,
so much trauma had been done to their bodies and psyches. And the
still uncalculated cost to those who survived such traumas—both in
the post-slavery diaspora and in the new postcolonial "independent"
nations—meant among other things displacement and an utterly profound change in their orientation to the world.

This change in orientation to the world is what I have called, trans-
lating ancient phenomena and dynamics into modern-world phenomena and dynamics, *contemptus mundi*[6]—a shorthand expression of
critical comparative historical orientation and ideology that can place

Achebe's Umuofia and other such peoples within larger historical and comparative dynamics, currents, and perspective. With *contemptus mundi* I try to capture part of the historical complex of responses from around the world to displacement, loss, and persistent humiliation and alienation. *Contemptus mundi* can be registered in several different keys, on several different levels. It is representation both for a historical literary expression and a worldview, with its associated politics and social orientation. There is a difference between the origins and uses of the expression *contemptus mundi* in a particular historical discursive situation and the longer and ongoing ideology/ideologization, orientation, and worldview often captured by the expression. As a rhetorical and literary expression, *contemptus mundi* is notably first associated with a type of literature that developed in the late Middle Ages in Europe, particularly in the eleventh and twelfth centuries, even as it drew on earlier rhetorics and texts that represent the widespread cultivation of the expression.[7] As shorthand for worldview and social orientation, *contemptus mundi* can be traced back to some philosophers and seers of the ancient Far East and the eastern Mediterranean and is associated with a range of responses to the world as challenges to and restructurings of the world.[8]

A modern trope or symbol that might in other words resignify *contemptus mundi* as a response to the modern world is the runaway or maroon. Marronage physical and psychical, or from the physical to psychical, captures the tradition in the black diaspora. Here literary critic Houston Baker, drawing on the arguments of Alain Locke and the artistry of Romare Bearden, has been provocative in associating those black folks who were part of the great migration tradition in the early to mid-twentieth century United States with those maroons who escaped from situations of Atlantic world slavery and with ongoing forms of social-cultural resistance and negotiation.[9]

I understand the ideology and politics of *contemptus mundi* and marronage to be discursive and analytical bridges to Achebe's things falling apart theme as a reading of the situation in Umuofia and, by extension, an independent Nigeria being born, and by further extension, the modern situation for black peoples throughout the world.

I also understand many other modern-world black African and African diaspora thinkers, writers, artists, and political and social and intellectual leaders and just ordinary folks to be in some respects in conversation with Achebe in terms of his reading. So I should like to evoke some of these figures and some of their sentiments and arguments having to do with modern black life and the shape of consciousness, of subjectivity, orientation to the world that Achebe's theme of things falling apart anticipates, translates, and channels. The attempt made here is to provide only a brief discussion of some registrations—other themes, symbols, tropes, images—of some modern black-inflected sentiments about how far things have fallen apart and what implications and ramifications therefrom are registered or begged.[10]

First, the "underground" as a motif rings a loud bell: I am reminded of the registration of the general attitude to the world and the need for escape from it as sedimented in modern urban U.S. black history and culture, from the heaviness of the struggles during slavery to the fairly light and sugary genres of pop music in the mid- to late twentieth century. A rather interesting example—the pop single of 1972, "People Make the World Go Round," sung by the Stylistics and written by Linda Creed and Thom Bell—makes the point and with it points to a bridge to popular discourse. According to the song, the world—especially that part that is the hustling, bustling inner-city—is to be viewed skeptically and warily because it is shaped by routinely inane if not insane activities and practices that go on and on—round and round, like a carousel—without reflection.[11] Peoples' heads are changed, or manipulated—they seem unable to see reality as it is. It is the wiser course, the songsters advise, to grab one's hat and *flee*—go "underground." In this obviously urban-centered, urban-inspired complaint, its oddly fast if not upbeat tempo—a kind of monotonous thumping, mimicking perhaps the simple, repetitive sounds one might hear at a fair, a carnival, or a circus at which clowns might appear—is placed squarely and paradoxically against the decidedly downbeat message, in which bad things happen. These bad things happen over and over again; they do not change; like a carousel, they go round and round.

The demographic reach or application of the situation bemoaned is made totally clear. Given the urban-specific foibles intoned, the situation certainly includes black urban life, but it is not clear that it is *only* about black life. Yet few would deny or argue against the assumption that the rhythms and syncopations and the misery-indexing rather dramatically mark modern black urban life in the United States. The veiling of the lyrics notwithstanding, they were likely meant to be a powerful and poignant baseline of human existence and struggle. So listeners are presented with a paean to the stressful life experienced through the prism of black-inflected urban life.

The theme of flight or escape is unmistakable in expressions about African American historical experiences. Every student of African American history understands the significance of the idea and stories of escape—from the era of slavery to the regime of Jim Crow to the more recent decades of multidirectional and multigenerational migrations and immigrations. The underground became the most important reference to the widespread network of peoples—in the early to mid-nineteenth century—involved in helping slaves escape to safe places in the northern United States and Canada. Nevertheless, the term can, and has often been expanded to, include reference to ongoing physical as well as psychological, social-cultural, and political-ideological flights or escapes from humiliating or stressful or debilitating or physically violent situations.[12]

So "People Make the World Go Round" simply appears to be one of so many interesting examples of refractions of the motif of black escape from trauma, and as such can serve as a cultural-discursive bridge between Achebe's black African-colonial-situated theme of things falling apart and the black diaspora-situated theme of things, shall we say, having devolved to a point that marronage—flight, into swamps or the underground (north)—suggests itself as being for many quite necessary. The song is part of a language or code that reflects the reality of the world holding the black self when not in physical bondage, certainly, in contempt, with the ensuing persistent warfare against and humiliation and repression of the black psyche and body. There is felt the pressing need to get out of harm's way and when and where possible to resist by any means possible. The histories of black communities on both sides of the Atlantic can be read as efforts to make sense of, to think through and come to speech about, to ideologize, this situation of black humiliation and escape from it into another world—the world of the underground. The themes of things falling apart (requiring some sort of escape) and that of the underground (assuming things have fallen apart) are pervasive among and I suggest define Black Atlantic worlds.

A now-classic translation and problematization of the themes and problems at issue having to do with black peoples' complex responses to humiliation can be found in Frederick Douglass's first autobiography, his 1845 *Narrative of the Life of Frederick Douglass an American Slave*.[13] A couple of incidents provide a wide and, I think, disturbing portal into black diaspora efforts to work through the issues and problems of black life falling apart and how the concept and experience of flight or escape are registered in it. Another look at this portal helps to make use of, to expand on, the rich texture of Achebe's novel and the note it strikes, for the sake of relating it to and thereby approaching a more complex sense of the expressivities and orientations that mark Black Atlantic history.[14]

The writerly Douglass looks back on an incident from his youth when he was a slave. The incident he reports was likely a recurring one, but he makes it read like a singular pointed incident for the sake of heightened narratological effect. It is an incident that Douglass remembers and recounts for his (assumed mostly) white abolitionist-minded readers. He seems to want to translate for them something about his (and other black folks') consciousness. What he touches upon and opens up in an astonishing display of a mix of romanticist and critical-reflexive communication are several issues that likely escaped the review of, or were not fully (or could not be fully) understood by, the Garrisonians, the abolitionist patron(izer)s of the young ex-slave.[15] These were issues that offered disturbing reports and incidents and challenges to his readers seemingly interested in learning something of the mind and inner world of the enslaved. Douglass doubtless provided more than any typical white reader would have expected.

The famous and riveting incident teaches us about that problem as well as much, much more—about thinking about thinking and apprehension through and in relationship to the sentiments and experiences of the enslaved and formerly enslaved:

> The slaves selected to go to the Great House Farm, for the monthly allowance for themselves and their fellow-slaves ... would make the dense woods, for miles around, reverberate with their wild songs, revealing at once the highest joy and the deepest sadness. They would compose and sing as they went along, consulting neither time nor tune. The thought that came up, came out—if not in the word, in the sound; and—as frequently in the one as in the other. They would sometimes sing the most pathetic sentiment in the most rapturous tone, and the most rapturous sentiment in the most pathetic tone. Into all of their songs they would manage to weave something of the Great House Farm. Especially would they do this, when leaving home. They would then sing most exultingly ... words which to many would seem *unmeaning jargon*, but which, nevertheless, were full of meaning to themselves ...
> I did not, when a slave, understand the deep meaning of those rude and apparently incoherent songs. I was myself within the circle; so that I neither saw nor heard as those without might see and hear.[16]

Douglass here names, I argue, in the other words I shall use, many issues for consideration—subjectivity and consciousness; discourse and power; power and knowledge; knowledge and positionality; knowledge and the center; knowledge and centers. He names or otherwise assumes at least three different categories of persons or groups as figures of different types of knowers or interpreters produced by the dense and tense world of slavocracy, often thought about in scholarly literature in the hyper-euphonious and politically uncharged language as "first contact."

First, there were the slave singers, who through their songs provide evidence that they had some knowledge and some agency of communication, but were nonetheless not allowed to communicate freely and widely their knowledge and sentiment beyond their own circle. Second, there were those outside the "circle" (of the slaves), the dominant world associated with the Great House Farm and all that it represents, and all other reality associated with it in codependency, including all those who, if they hear the slave songs at all, hear them only as jargon, as "mumbo jumbo."[17] And third, Douglass himself who, although technically (in narratological time) "within the circle," did not/could not know much more than the other slaves. But later, as reflected by his writerly self, outside the narratological frame and outside the circle of the enslaved, he paradoxically begins to think about not only what the slaves felt and communicated in that experience he finds himself removed from, but also something more, something about communicating, about knowing in general, something made all the more poignant and heavy, all the more urgent and pressing, all the more real and relevant by the alternations of the circumstances and slavery and freedom.

So using the situation of black slaves—including his memory of his own slave self—to think with, Douglass thinks in terms of "site" sanctioning "insight,"[18] that is, in terms of types of consciousness and interpretations and the corresponding interpreters who are differently positioned—the enslaving; the enslaved; and the runagate. This three-part schema of types of consciousness that I isolate in Douglass's narrative may be seen to correspond to an extent to two of the stages or dynamics in my scripturalectics schema as types of consciousness/ways of knowing that structure this book. His first two types—the enslaving and the enslaved—may be argued to correspond to my second turn in scripturalectics, having to do with a type of (self-) enslavement. His third type—the runagate—corresponds to my third reading, having to do with efforts to problematize and escape the effects of the violent imposition that is slavery. I think it important to include discussion of Douglass's narrative here in this chapter because the narrative is best understood as advancing if not actually constructing a discourse about the black enslaved that is by definition so dire that "things falling apart" might be characterized as being an example of euphemy. The types of consciousness I tease out of Douglass's narrative, I submit, are not always totally mutually exclusive. They can be, and in history and in individuals and among groups have been, complexly intertwined. Yet there is justification for their isolation for the sake of critical analysis of the dynamics of consciousness. There is no escape from the consequences set in motion by that contact that was turned into violent conquest and long-term dominance for some, and long-term subordination and humiliation for many others.

Douglass's analysis begins—complexly, emotionally—with those whose very identity as human agents was questioned and denied. This means he, like all those on the periphery, can and must take into consideration the whole situation having to do with human types and stages in consciousness. So he begins with black enslavement as a way to the problematization of what Houston Baker, following on the work of Stephen Henderson, called the "black (w)hole,"[19] a profound understanding of black existence in terms of darkness fathomed, embraced, used in order to find healing and wholeness. To the three categories of consciousness/interpretation found in Douglass's now famous story I briefly turn.

First, *the enslaving*. Those participating in and profiting from the structure of dominance generated by the Great House Farm were understood by Douglass to be oblivious to the plight of others. They are imagined to be those who, like Equiano in mimicking white men with weaponized scriptures (as we discussed in Chapter 2), or the buzzards in Robert Penn Warren's "Pondy Woods" lifting their wings so as to avoid seeing and hearing the black runaway, are the black Others not countenanced, not seen or heard (except to be *over*heard, *over*seen, *over*determined).[20] Those of the Great House Farm around the world might also be characterized, according to Frantz Fanon, as those who show that they have fallen prey to the Manichean psychology and epistemics that constructed and then overdetermined colonial structures and populations: The world was understood to be black and white, the latter signifying light and purity and life, the former dirt and pollution.[21] Of course, we now know more about what subtends such psychology and epistemics: We know now that the polarity represents a horrific splitting of the self, into something like the blankness of whiteness and the foreboding, threatening, radical markedness of blackness. The splitting is traumatic; it is rarely recognized or acknowledged; it is part of the phenomenon of what some scientists have called the "hidden brain."[22] Among other things, it results in the meta-racist regime or syndrome that makes all of us carry the lies, pollutes all of us, infects our discourses and all the domains of our work and play, including our academic and intellectual, social and religious, civic and political, capitalistic and professional games.

This Manichean syndrome was at work in Jefferson's convoluted denial of Phillis Wheatley's brilliant artistry.[23] It was there in Hegel's disavowal of and profound and eerie silence about the successful struggle of those black folk in Saint Domingue-turned-Haiti against their enslavers and the meaning of such struggle as the backdrop for his own theorizing about the dialectics of struggle between master and slave and the meaning of this struggle for the development of the concept of universalism and the turn to modernity.[24] It was evident in John Locke's "purification of language" project, part of the "meta-discursive formation" aimed to deny the right to public speech to anyone—women, serfs and slaves, sub-aristocratic whites—who could not speak properly (that is, like a properly socialized white man).[25] It was at work when Tony Perkins, the head of the evangelical and corporatist Family Research Council, declared on CNN in the heat of the 2008 presidential election—that election that threatened and in fact did result in the election of the first nonwhite person as president of the United States—with great authority and without a whiff of qualification that the *jeremiads* of the urban black pastor named *Jeremiah* Wright against corporatist and racializing/racist "America" were simply "unscriptural."[26] Can we doubt that Perkins's utterance comes out of the still regnant colonial-turned-Manichean world? Is it hard to see that in Perkins's mind—buried far in that hidden brain where meta-racism thrives—there is an assumption that he and his tribesmen alone own, and remain the authorized managers of interpretation of or discourses about, the Bible and all other legitimate cultural script(ure)s? Who cannot see that behind his outburst were social-cultural or racialist presumptions often legitimized by the feigned apolitical silences and stances of scholarly guilds that conjure the ancient Near Eastern or biblical world as a white world in seamless historical development with the modern white or Euro-American world? Such disavowals and tortured silences and twisted arguments and declarations and arguments reflect the pollution and toxicity—what W. E. B. Du Bois calls the "veiling" of consciousness—that is the hallmark of the Manichean psychology and epistemics, infecting all of us.[27]

One measuring stick—the rhetorics of the 2016 presidential election campaign suggest that it may no longer be possible for any of us—the powerful and the humiliated—all subject to the Manichean construction or regime to argue freely what we see, think, or feel. Having to make "black" and—in the wake of the dyspeptic and violent 2016 campaign rhetorics about illegal immigration—"brown" always signify the negative ("rapists," "murderers") represents a tremendous burden for free and clear thinking. I suspect that, contrary to views expressed, Donald Trump's rapid-fire, no-holds-barred, shoot-from-the-hip rhetoric may actually be more burdensome for him than he lets on. As I write this book I take note of views of Trump as free and unconstrained big man who tells it like it is, an anti-establishment figure and force immune to the pressures of political correctness, I detect something quite different: I hear and read his imprisonment in the tight and imprisoning discourse he has stepped into and ratcheted up. The care that must be taken to hide the truth and tell only certain lies in certain ways must be very onerous, indeed.[28]

So, who enslaves whom? Frederick Douglass implied that those far outside the circle—those of the Great House Farm who, like the woman in Lafitau's frontispiece (see Figure 2.1), representing Euro-America or the West writing up the Rest who are made unable to see or hear, much less understand—hardly acknowledge the humanity and sensibilities of the Others. Their gazes are fixed, straight in their focus. Like the poignantly named Nehemiah who "writes up" Dessa in Sherley Williams's *Dessa Rose*,[29] the dominants make up a "science," writing (scriptures) that represents a kind of violence done to the other's body.[30]

Are those who enslave and write up the Others not also ensnared? Or is this too easy and fancy a manipulation of the word and the historical situations? Ought we not consider what the look straight ahead or the silence means or portends? Might the look straight ahead—the Manichean gaze—without at first intending to see others eventually develop into a chronic inability to see others or to read nuance or around the corners or the play and texture that marks so much of human life? Whatever we may determine to be the moral implications of colonial domination and slavery and humiliation of the other, we should also consider the significant effect these forms of violence have on the perpetrators. So much violence, such limited range for free thinking.

Second, *the enslaved.* In Douglass's view they seemed to have been denied any but overdetermined identification with and participation in the world that was controlled by the Great House Farm. They appeared to have been denied the main currents of communication and social exchange. They were considered chattel, and so it was assumed that they were unable to think, to communicate, except in the way of the "swinish multitude."[31] They were presumed not to be able to read and write—at least, not in canonical/cosmopolitan European languages or modes.[32]

But these assumptions and conclusions were themselves part of the power of the world of the Great House Farm—the power, that is, to signify and label and codify. Even as the mature writerly Douglass comes to speech, his rather unstable positionality and consciousness are made evident in the halting language about the situation. Douglass knew that the black enslaved could indeed make meaning or make things mean, could communicate with one another. It was he who, as he remembered the situation, seemed outside their circle of communication, and being outside of their circle, they seemed to him—because he could not understand what meanings they were conveying—to lack intersubjectivity. But this likely was not only his youthful ignorance; it also lined up with the ideology of the Great House Farm because it was the ideological stance required for maintenance of dominance. This ideology also likely created and exacerbated in Douglass what might be thought of as "anxiety of ethnicity,"[33] a splitting, a crisis of identity of a sort. Who does not generally want to be associated with (the group that reflects) knowledge and power? I fear little contradiction in stating that among African Americans this anxiety continues to be acutely and painfully felt.

What Douglass here complexly and disturbingly registered was the sentiment of the (word of the) Great House Farm about those it enslaved—that the latter had no language to be respected.[34] Slaves' communication was reduced to an "anti-language,"[35] unrecognized and unacknowledged by others. This is what Douglass called "unmeaning jargon." Black peoples who had been slaves were rendered silent and invisible. Ralph Ellison's character in *Invisible Man* put the phenomenon in the now-famous riveting terms:

> I am invisible . . . simply because people refuse to see me. Like the bodiless heads you see sometimes in circus sideshows, it is as though I have been surrounded by mirrors of hard, distorting glass . . . they see only my surroundings, themselves, or figments of their imagination—indeed, everything and anything except me.[36]

The evidence of the silencing of and rendering invisible the Black Atlantic is ironically everywhere to be seen. One might conclude that modern Euro-American worlds were obviously built on efforts to keep black peoples silent and invisible, broken. And, of course, such efforts have always been just as quickly and obviously denied.[37]

Perhaps the most famous description, if not the final analysis, of the phenomenon of the enslaved as the framed is found in Du Bois's works. In his *The Souls of Black Folk*, the Manichean world, the world structured around what he termed the "veil," is defined by racial division and alienation and ignorance—the color line—that pollutes all.[38] One might be tempted to argue that these words are dripping in hyperbole—except that since these words were written, our history again and again has made them disturbingly prophetic.

As Douglass looked back to the Great House Farm he indicates that he had come to understand that the chief dilemma that slaves faced was not the physical domination, as demeaning as it was, but the not being seen, not being heard, not being understood, not being free to communicate in broad terms befitting the dignity of humanity, not being able to communicate the complexity of sentiments and feelings, and being cut off from everything—except, ironically, the Great House Farm. Circumstances might allow some singing among slaves, but only within bounds, within the Manichean-prescribed circle in which black was associated with, among other things, "unmeaning jargon." This was for Douglass an intolerable situation. He escaped it. This escape was not marronage on a grand scale in terms of participation with large numbers and in terms of miles traversed, but in terms of the depth of change in the psyche and emotions it was radical.

Third, *the Runagate*. This term is an alternate form of "renegate," from Middle Latin *renegatus*, meaning "fugitive" or "runaway." In black diaspora literature and expressivity, it has come to carry the meaning of a decidedly transgressive act, having to do with marronage, running away with an attitude and a plan, a taking flight—in body, but even more importantly in terms of consciousness.[39]

We know that Douglass literally runs away from enslavement. It is as a runagate that he writes his first autobiography (first version). And in the recounting of the story about the slaves on their way to the Great House Farm the reader is conditioned to see Douglass as one already set apart—clearly in terms of his being of *writerly* consciousness—from the others who are slaves. He is figured as one both in and out of solidarity with the slaves but sometimes and in some respects sharing consciousness with them. He knows them, but he is also alien to them. That he once occupied a somewhat similar psychic position to them, but even more so later as a public speaker and writer was rather differently positioned from them, makes his writerly positionality and orientation excruciatingly torturous for him. He registers acute anxiety over the need to step outside the circle, outside the framed experience and framed consciousness that is slavery. Where he now as writer finds himself is a scary place. It is psychosocial and discursive marronage. He was a runagate of a sort *before* he ran away.

As I mentioned briefly above, in the context of discussion about *contemptus mundi* and marronage, there is a long history of this phenomenon of the runagate—long before and long after Douglass—among the people who have become and whom we now call African Americans (but here now necessarily meaning Africans throughout the Americas). The runagate involved not only heroic individuals, such as Douglass, but everyday collective folk who showed themselves to be a people on the run, a marooned people, a people intent on migrating from deserts and fields of enslavement to other psychic places, with high purpose. So what I think must be emphasized in this context of discussion is the (other) purpose of flight, how it was used to help make a world.

Taking flight, running away, was considered by some of my relatives in the early to mid-twentieth century. Some decided to move themselves to the cities—southern and northern—away from dire and threatening situations. They were in search of something different, something better for their economic and physical and psychic health—and their dignity. In his now-famous 1925 edited volume *The New Negro: Voices of the Harlem Renaissance*, Alain Locke vividly captured the impetus and drama of the waves of migration in the twentieth century, of which some of my relatives were part:

> The wash and rush of this human tide ... is to be explained primarily in terms of a new vision of opportunity, of social and economic freedom, of a spirit to seize, even in the face of an extortionate and heavy toll ... With each successive wave of it, the *movement* of the Negro becomes more and more a mass *movement* toward the larger and the more democratic chance ... a deliberate flight not only from the countryside to city, but from medieval America to modern.[40]

More recently, journalist Isabel Wilkerson, in her highly acclaimed book *Warmth of Other Suns: The Epic Story of America's Great Migration* (2010), revisited this phenomenon from another perspective and through another genre, with her vivid storytelling about individuals and families and their profound experiences. Her argument about the larger meanings of the movements is in conversation with Douglass and many others who had escaped:

> the common denominator for leaving was the desire to be free, like the Declaration of Independence said, free to try out for most any job they pleased, play checkers with whomever they chose, sit where they wished on the streetcar, watch their children walk across the stage for the degree most of them didn't have the chance to get. They left to pursue some version of happiness, whether they achieved it or not. It was a seemingly simple thing that the majority of Americans could take for granted but the migrants and their forebears never had a right to in the world they had fled.[41]

Douglass, like the twentieth-century migrants, escaped in order to be free and to pursue his own understanding of happiness. The forces that held Douglass also obtained—with a few changes in protocol—well into the twentieth century.[42] Following Douglass, with his heightened consciousness and facility for writing, is critical here. He may not be in many respects "perfectly" representative of those who had been enslaved, but in terms of the focal experience—of humiliation and degradation—and the complex responses to it, he thinks/feels and speaks/writes for the many. This includes his still haunting and liberating expression of sentiments and identification of forms of articulation of experience.

The critical sign of Douglass having already become a runagate before reaching the North is his acquisition and critical use of literacy. Learning to read had to do with more than learning the letters, having being given the "inch," as he called it. No, his reading involved much more than learning letters; it had to do with taking steps in agency and conscientization that were much feared by the masters. Douglass's command of the text is like Maurice Blanchot's notion of reading past the text to something more, a reading of the self—a historicized collective self.[43] This self that Douglass began to "read" seems to be the result of a splitting of a different sort from, but with great implications and ramifications for, the engagement of the Manichean psychology that structured the psychosocial logic of the slaveholding North Atlantic worlds.

Again, Du Bois provides perspective on the matter. His references in *Souls* to the term "veil" as metaphor to name the nature of the construction of the Manichean world, and his understanding of the consequences and impact of such, include that most famous remark about black existence in the United States: "a peculiar sensation … double-consciousness, this sense of always looking at one's self through the eyes of the others."[44] This remark is generally assumed to apply simply and universally to all black peoples in the United States. This interpretation is questionable as applied to *Souls*: In the latter Du Bois was focused on explaining (to a racially mixed readership) those black folks who were physically and increasingly psychically removed from the world of the Great House Farm and were now facing the challenge of negotiation of larger miscegenated worlds and consciousness. Du Bois understood that for such persons—like himself and like Douglass "outside the circle"—what was experienced most acutely is a splitting, an acute self-alienation, dissociation. This was what he termed existence behind the "Veil of Color."[45]

Back to Douglass: Another incident from his story is relevant here and will throw light on some of the lingering questions. His miscegenated and alienated consciousness led him to wage battle with Covey, the infamous "nigger-breaker." It was seemingly only a physical battle, but much more was involved: What was also reflected was Douglass's deeper struggle with alienation and anxiety in the world. In Covey, Douglass comes face to face, so to speak, with the more tangible manifestations of meta-racism—the slave system and its imbrication of Christian ideology, as well as its control of social and political constructs and construction. This framing ideology in all social domains and sectors also occasioned and forced the opportunity for Douglass to represent his confrontation with—or better, his critical engagement of—the world of the slave, more specifically African (folk) traditions, translated by Sandy, the local root doctor. The testing of the powers, the strange "magic," of the "African" or African diaspora worlds over against or certainly in relationship to the "magic"—no less the strange operations and constructions—of the white world, seemed necessary. Douglass was thereby put in such a tight and suffocating ideological-discursive and physical space. How could it be otherwise? Like Jacob's wrestling with the angel, Douglass fights a multipronged, multileveled existential battle. He fights against the meta-racism that frames every-thing around him, including language and aspects of the self that have been forced to split on account of Manichean meta-racism. He fights the white side of himself, represented by Covey (and his absent father), which derides and demeans and denies him and his blackness. And he fights the black side of himself, represented by Sandy, with his transla-tion of African and African-diaspora traditions, sadly also mixed with his own personal cowardice and perfidy.

Douglass shows himself to be conscious of the tightly coiled con-structedness of these worlds. In the end, his fight with Covey is a stand-in or sign of his wrestling with all these worlds and their challenges, their holds on him. His facing Covey, not necessarily his whipping Covey, was his victory: It results in his becoming a free miscegenated subject, not merely a blending in crude literal/physical terms, but in terms of an independent self that is unstable, fluid, protean, embattled, split from the tight, toxic, convoluted violent framings:

This battle with Mr. Covey was the turning-point in my career as a slave. It rekindled the few expiring embers of freedom, and revived within me a sense of my own manhood. It recalled the departed self-confidence, and inspired me again with a determination to be free. The gratification afforded me by the triumph was a full compensation for whatever else might follow, even death itself. He only can understand the deep satisfaction which I experience, who has himself repelled by force the bloody arm of slavery. I felt as I never felt before. It was a *glorious resurrection*, for the tomb of slavery, to the heaven of free-dom. My long-crushed spirit rose, cowardice departed, bold defiance took its place; and now I resolved that, however long I might remain a slave *in form*, the day has passed forever when I could be a slave *in fact*. I did not hesitate to let it be known of me, that the white man who expected to succeed in whipping me, must also succeed in killing me.[46] (emphases mine)

As his recounting and interpretation of the incident make clear, Douglass's life was forever changed. As my emphases above suggest, it was his registration of his attitude toward death that was key. That is, as Douglass faced Covey he was facing death—or facing his willingness to die in order to come alive, experience "resurrection." Everything turned around the distinction he made between a slave either "in fact" or "in form." The latter referred to being in literal chains—whatever the disposition of the one in chains; the former referred to the disposition—fear, of death—that really makes one a slave. Fear of Covey and failure to confront him makes one a slave *in fact*. Facing Covey and all that Covey represents made him a slave (only) *in form*.

In his brilliant analysis of what he terms his "archaeology of death," literary critic Abdul R. JanMohamed identifies in Richard Wright's works a "dialectic of death" in relationship to the death-bound subject that he argues Wright defines as the modern black subject. Drawing on the arguments and theoretics of Hegel, Heidegger, and the sociologist Orlando Patterson, among a few others, JanMohamed lays out the turns in this dialectic:

1. Baseline: slave status
2. Thesis: "social death," what he and Patterson understand to be the chief and perduring condition and effect (excruciating alienation) of chattel slavery of the sort that most black peoples in the Americas had to undergo
3. Antithesis: "actual death"—following Heidegger's notion of "demising," the biological death of the subject, in which the subject is well aware of his dying, which in turn must be seen as an eventuality of his choosing (thus, the precondition for the slave's social death)
4. (Potential) Synthesis: "symbolic death"—the death of the slave as one who was socially dead, and the rebirth into a different subjectivity (even as the other threats remain). JanMohamed in fact uses Douglass's account of his "resurrection" experience in

the wake of his fight with Covey as the most "graphic example" of the most difficult condition to experience—"symbolic death."[47]

Here we have a theoretical-analytical handle on what could be termed Douglass's serious theorizing about death as a way to think about modern black life. In terms beyond strict chronological anteriority, Douglass anticipates and joins Achebe in conversation about "things falling apart" as shorthand for death and as a marker of modern black existence. A strong connection between Achebe's and Douglass's views about black life and violence and death can be seen (1) in Okonkwo's suicide as example of actual death; (2) in the Umuofian villagers' conversion to white men's religion as ongoing social death; and (3) in the courage and steadiness, engagement and criticism, the honest declaration about the fate of the world of Umuofia, all associated with Obierika, as symbolic death. And it seems hard to deny that Wright was not channeling Douglass in the way in which Wright wrote about violence and death in black life.[48] What were Bigger Thomas and Fred Daniels saying about (black) life, if not that it was all about violence and death—and about the need to face it, throw oneself into it, to show it to be what it is in the world?

Douglass provides a riveting account of his resurrection, his facing and defying and living with death, to be sure. But he is in his story rather heroic; his story does not read like a story for all, or the life all can live. Most of us may approach or experience life much more like Sandy—mostly stuck, tortured, from moment to moment strategic in our thinking for the sake of survival, twisting in the torturous and violent cross-winds of social death. To the extent that the embracing of symbolic death is understood to be the goal to achieve, most of us may fall short, unsure how to reach it. Douglass provides the story that shows that we might face, and how we might face (or not face), actual death in any moment. There is striking evidence in the civil rights struggle in the United States and in the independence movements in Africa (and before and after, in so many situations that are not and probably never will be chronicled for us) that some have been willing to face actual death precisely for the sake of the overthrow of persistent social death (registered in slavery, Jim Crowism, colonialism). But Douglass's story, of his death and resurrection, in its various iterations, and notwithstanding its inspirational and provocative nature, probably cannot be—should it be?—considered a guide for all to follow. Is (the writerly) Douglass too heroic for our own good? What happened to the other Great House Farm slaves? And, perhaps as important, what was the life of their "unmeaning jargon"? What sort of death did they continue to experience? And how did their "jargon" communicate this experience? No follow-through, no answers, from Douglass.

In Achebe's story we are not given that much more, if as much: There is no subtlety in the message that Okonkwo provides no way out for those who were his kinsmen, or for the readers of the story. How many actual deaths by our own hand can we afford? How much mimetics—in Christian, Muslim, or vague Africentric form—is required for the African diaspora to stay socially dead, albeit alive? With Obierika as representative of the survivors facing scripturalization as a type of violence and social death, there is no real plan offered, no guidance provided, no source of knowledge or knowing pointed to, no strategic vision or orientation. Even Achebe's sequel novels seem only—does art here imitate life?—to show how things fall apart even more deeply and tragically, not so much how survivors fare and escape and thrive. Yet the persistence of the motif of things falling apart and related themes—in Achebe's work and in others—is worth continuing attention and engagement.

JanMohamed's wide-ranging and deep analysis of Wright's work notwithstanding, it leaves out of consideration a work of Wright that I think (as does JanMahomed in confession[49]) is in fact most important for a discussion of Wright's views of death, in particular about the terms on which the conceptualization and ongoing orientation to and politics around symbolic death might be advanced. In short, neither Douglass nor Achebe helped readers understand what it means to live a life—with what consciousness, politics, orientation?—of symbolic death. Wright's work revives and expands the focus and challenge. In point of fact, this focus may very well be Wright's enduring challenge and contribution as writer.

The work I have in mind is Wright's novella "The Man Who Went Underground" (hereafter "Underground").[50] First published in 1944, amid the shocks and traumas that mark World War II, "Underground" centers on a character whose plight seems to reflect where Umuofia is left after the suicide of Okonkwo—with the challenge of figuring out responses adequate to the negotiation of an incomprehensible and hostile world. In this and in his other works—especially novels—Wright as much as, if not more than, any other Black Atlantic writer, presents us with a violent, death-riddled, dark world experienced by dark peoples.

The main character of "Underground," like so many black diaspora individuals of stories, texts, and films, is depicted as an alien, a stranger to self and in the world, one who is made invisible and mute (73, 74). Not at the beginning but later in the story the character is identified strangely as "freddaniels."[51] This odd way of introducing and registering the character's name—typed out on a typewriter as one of the several examples of odd things discovered in the underground—signifies strongly and I think multivalently.

The story at first blush turns around the not-so-odd Fred Daniels— a married city dweller with children—who finds himself detained by the police and accused of the murder of a white woman. He is now made a black man: He is put under enormous pressure of the sort that our news headlines today vividly and now unsurprisingly register as urban policing's efficient application to black males. The pressure of the police officers was applied to Fred Daniels until, out of exhaustion, he confesses to the murder. Things here also begin quickly and irrevocably to fall apart: In fact, they seem to proceed according to a scenario quite familiar to black peoples in relationship to law enforcement in the United States. That is, until Daniels escapes. He runs away in the same manner and for the same reasons that are captured so vividly by so many artists and thinkers, ideologists and activists throughout the history of African America. In the poem "Runagate, Runagate,"

Robert Hayden has woven together perhaps the classic expressions and images of black cultural sentiments regarding the runagate:[52]

I.
Runs falls rises stumbles on from darkness into darkness
and the darkness thicketed with shapes of terror
and the hunters pursuing and the hounds pursuing
and the night cold and the night long and the river
to cross and the jack-muh-lanterns beckoning beckoning
and blackness ahead and when shall I reach that somewhere
morning and keep on going and never turn back and keep
   on going
       Runagate
          Runagate
           Runagate
. . .

  II.
. . .

Wanted   Harriet Tubman   alias The General
alias Moses   Stealer of Slaves

In league with Garrison   Alcott   Emerson
Garrett   Douglas   Thoreau   John Brown

Armed and known to be Dangerous

Wanted   Reward   Dead or Alive

   . . .

Come ride-a my train
Oh that train, ghost-story train
through swamp and savanna movering movering,
over trestles of dew, through caves of the wish,
Midnight Special on a sabre track movering movering,
  . . .

136

Come ride-a my train

Mean mean mean to be free

On the run in the city, Daniels sees a manhole and makes use of it to go into the sewer system, the underground. It is his experience of the underground—a dark and dank place—that opens Daniels up to a different view and perspective—a double-sightedness that paradoxically represented a heightened and more expansive and enlightened consciousness, even if it also reflected the somewhat irrational, the impulsive, the ethically and morally unstable, the volatile and the ambiguous. He has experiences with certain things (money, guns, watches, diamonds, a radio, a typewriter) and groups (the church) from this new position(ality) that make them seem strange. They were all on the same level of value for him, "the serious toys of the men who lived in the dead world of sunshine and rain he had left, the world that had condemned him" (47). He loses a sense of time, of memory of events and persons; and he forgets the uses of things. He feels anxious, dreadful, alone, and lonely but also at times ecstatic. The reasons for the former are clear and obvious: He is a man who has been made a stranger in the world and to himself, a man made socially dead. The reason for the latter is more complicated—it has to do with the work he makes the underground experience do for him.

Wright made the underground space in which Fred Daniels comes to a point of committing himself to facing actual death. He is willing to confront the police. This resolve comes about after the story makes clear that Daniels undergoes a transformation such that he sees/knows/feels differently everything with which he comes into contact. What provokes this difference is a change in consciousness or orientation, a deepening of reflection, the mimetic excess referenced above. The latter allowed him to split and so to see himself outside himself. Given this experience, things simply did not mean in the same way:

> He stood in the dark, wet with sweat, brooding about the diamonds, the rings, the watches, the money; he remembered the singing in the church, the people yelling in the movie, the dead baby, the nude man stretched

out upon the white table . . . He saw these items hovering before his eyes and felt that some dim meaning linked them together . . . He stared with vacant eyes, convinced that all of these images, with their tongueless reality, were striving to tell him something. (51)

He experienced people and their doings as taking place "on some far-off planet" (52); most dynamics appeared to be part of a game (53). Or worse, "the world aboveground . . . seemed to him, *a wild forest filled with death*" (54, my emphasis).

One of the most important scenes in the novella depicts Daniels after some time spent playing with diamonds in a jewelry store he had accessed from the underground. It is a scene that provides the reader access to Daniels's mind and through the narrator to a major point of the story:

He stooped and flung the diamonds more evenly over the floor and they showered rich sparks, collaborating with him. He went over the floor and trampled the stones just deep enough for them to be fairly visible, as though they were set delicately in the prongs of a thousand rings. A ghostly light bathed the cave. He sat on the chest and frowned. Maybe anything's right, he mumbled. Yes, if the world as men had made it was right, then *any*thing else was right, any act a man took to satisfy himself, murder, theft, torture. (56)

I find this to be a rather astounding passage. It captures Daniels's/ Wright's orientation to the world and consciousness. Orientation and consciousness are determined by and reflected back onto the experience of the "world as men had made it." The latter is clearly the world that holds Daniels in contempt, chases him through the streets of the city, and forces him to confess to murder. The response—the orientation—is in turn contempt *for* that world.

It is this orientation that reflects freedom that correlates with symbolic death—that of a kind of mentality that sees reality as having fallen apart and "fallen out of history."[53] It is an attitude of radical skepticism, a questioning of reality as constructed. It opens up a world in which meaning and its structures and arrangements and protocols are no longer accepted. When one cannot explain oneself adequately to others, when one cannot make one's understandings of things "have the same meaning" (79), things have indeed fallen apart. Daniels understood that there was a great distance, an unbridgeable chasm, between what he felt and what others meant (72). His whole being was full of what he "wanted to say ... but he could not say it" (69). His speech was like that of a child who was experiencing a "dream" (70). He had difficulty finding words to communicate (74) his feelings.

In police custody again, the "old mood" he had felt in the underground "surged back". This feeling seems to have been understood to pertain to courage and resolve, so "He leaned forward and spoke eagerly" (70).

It is assumed that this misfiring—mishearing, misreading, misapprehension, the strange reaction—is what happens when things fall apart, when social relations are structured such that social death is experienced, but then overcome, and when actual death is faced. It involves working one's way into symbolic death. It is what symbolic death looks like by the Fred Daniels's of the world. With the acceptance of actual death, the facing of the ultimate fears ("I'll show you everything!"), Daniels came to understand what he had been experiencing—a type of freedom from his "burden" of guilt. What brings on this guilt is not made clear: He seems to think the churchgoers, for example, suffered much too much from it. This is not surprising emphasis from Wright, who as a child was made to undergo and hate the psychological weights the black church world put on him and his kind. But there seems to be a lightening of the load at the thought of the possibility of sharing with others the enlightenment realized. He seemed to feel a real need to communicate—"he had to make them believe him!" (75), to show the officers the dark sewer as a cave from which he had seen the light:

A mood of high selflessness throbbed in him. He could barely contain his rising spirits. They would see what he had seen; they would feel what he had felt. He would lead them through all the holes he had dug and ... He wanted to make a hymn, prance about in physical ecstasy, throw his arm about the police in fellowship. (80)

Recalling the song he had heard before in the church, he sings it softly, embraces it without criticism:

> Glad, glad, glad, oh, so glad
> I got Jesus in my soul ... (80)

Of course, this time the song for him is about connection, intimacy, consciousness, not guilt.

Daniels is now quite willing to sign another confession, even to die. He is without anxiety and care. There is no anger or rage. But there is the contempt for the world insofar as the underground brings joy, ecstasy, peace, release, and relief. From his experience underground, in seeing things from a different position and differently, seeing that there is no ruling logic, system, or structure—no (stable) meaning in the world structured by white peoples of the aboveground—that is independent of human ingenuity, scheming, politics, and foibles, Daniels is released. Now, he understands that anything goes, anything is possible. What is has been or can be constructed; this includes his self-construction and socialization. The activities and projects aboveground are essentially fakery, nonsensical.

Because Daniels's underground experience appears to others to be so odd, nonsensical behavior—"crazy talk," "he could not explain himself to them," "delusions of grandeur," "Maybe it's because he lives in a white man's world"—he questions the nature of human communication and expressivity. He now understands language not as a simple carrier of meaning; no, it seems to hide, to disturb, to defy meaning, to signify the rupture of meaning.

Here it seems appropriate, in order to gain perspective on Wright's construction of Daniels, to shift attention to a larger context of language use and meaning construction or loss by enslaved black peoples. Any consideration of black language and meaning should go through the door, so to speak, of the slave songs. And any reflection on the slave songs should be in conversation with Du Bois. In *Souls* Du Bois argued that along with "unmeaning rhapsody" the songs reflect uses of the Bible—"conventional theology"—and in such usage "concealed" "much of real poetry and meaning." The point here is that the concealment was not a simple lack; it was silence, but the silence was not the same as not communicating. On the contrary, this "silence" was part of a conscious deliberate strategy to communicate an ongoing fathoming of the abject self and that self in the world:

> Like all primitive folk, the slave stood near to Nature's heart. Life was a "rough and rolling sea" like the brown Atlantic of the Sea Islands, the "Wilderness" was the home of God, and the "lonesome valley" led to the way of life.... Over the inner thoughts of the slaves and their relations one with another the shadow of fear ever hung, so that we get but glimpses here and there ... *eloquent omissions and silences* (my emphasis).[54]

The function of the "omissions" and "silences" is made clearer in an essay by literary critic Houston Baker, "Lowground and Inaudible Valleys: Reflections on Afro-American Spirit Work."[55] Baker argues that the "silence" in black folk culture is best understood in terms of a holding back from normal/traditional uses of language, a turning away from the regular forms in order to express critique and healing. Drawing upon writer and critic Susan Sontag's essay on silence, Baker called for a "criticism of silence" to "match the depths of a magnificently enhancing black sounding of experience."[56] The silence, he argued, reflects the radical strategies of what he calls in his *Modernism and the Harlem Renaissance* "flight" or cultural "marronage," involving "veiling/masking," "mastery of form," and "deformation of mastery," for the sake of the survival and building of a nation.[57] This channels Toni Morrison's language about women's voices breaking "the back of words."[58] It also resonates powerfully with philosopher Susan Buck-Morss's provocative book *Hegel, Haiti, and Universal History*, in which she argues, drawing on literary critic Joan Dayan's equally provocative *Haiti, History, and the Gods*, that

African diaspora expressivities and orientation—reflected mostly in religious ritual—reflect the pummeling and violence, the ultimate loss and dispossession experienced, the "shreds of bodies come back," and the resultant "decay of meanings."[59] Baker eloquently summarizes the arguments and stakes: For black and subaltern critical consciousness, there is no meaning in any narrative, any script, any text, any tradition unless it is first ripped, broken and then "entranced," blackened—that is, made usable for the life underground:

> Merely arranged in a traditional ... problematic ... words are ineffectual. Only when they enter into entranced performance ... do they give birth to sounds of a new order.[60]

The entranced performance about which Baker speaks is realized only when there is an addressing of the "lowground and inaudible valleys"—the deepest reaches of the collective psyche and sentiment—of black folk. At such a point the canonical arrangements and structures that present themselves and with which black folk are forced to negotiate are exploded—into various expressions of contempt for the world and their politics.

With such *contemptus mundi* the veil is ripped, a tear obtains, even if not in absolute terms. There is flight, "escape," from harshness, from humiliation, from the incessant violence done them in Western canonical "history" that erases black folk and makes them invisible, mute, marginal. And the flight is registered in all sorts of ways and domains—from the physical and literal to the psychical and imaginary, crossing genres, generations. That is why the songs, as poignant examples of soundings, or as alternate speech, or a kind of silence, must *not* be set aside. In fact, they must be analyzed if the ascetics of (de-)formation are to be recognized and understood at all. The songs are sites of mimetic excess, the plenitude of free, liquid articulations of life in a world filled with contempt for the songsters:

> the music of an unhappy people, of the children of disappointment; they tell of death and suffering and unvoiced longing toward a truer world,

of misty wanderings and hidden ways ... of trouble and exile, of strife and hiding: they grope toward some unseen power and sigh for rest in the End . [61]

Might Wright's Fred Daniels have heard the (equivalent sentiments of the) slave songs in his head as he sang softly the song recalled from the church on his way to death? Might this version of song have been considered less the articulation of guilt, more the expression of *contemptus mundi*? Because Daniels's experience suggests it as a baseline explanation, I return to *contemptus mundi* and what and how it registers. What his experience in the underground registers is the orientation that is *contemptus mundi* in the diaspora as well as in the African colonial and postcolonial situation in terms of the loss, the decay, the death, of meaning. Down in the dark, the sewer, the Platonic cave in reverse, meaning died. What is meant here—what I mean here—is not merely anomie or indifference or apathy, certainly not that orientation that is reflective of what is often associated with an elitist and belated modernism or postmodernism, but something quite different, something much more layered and complicated.

No, *contemptus mundi* among the black dispossessed and humiliated in the modern world is more the registration of a kind of flight, silence, nonparticipation, a refusal, as it were, to play the discursive/ political/moral-ethical games played by dominants, especially the language game that is part of their regime. A world of meaning, after all, is impossible in a world in which the infrastructure of meaning-making itself is shattered, when black is so overdetermined that it renders thinking itself toxic. So *contemptus mundi* in such a circle means refusal to invest in, commit to, the dominant paradigm or regime in the way or on the terms expected. It represents a type of counter-play. It does not mean no play at all—as in paralysis. Such analysis is too simple, too flat, effecting a dangerous narrowing and coopting, fed by the long history of uncreative and narrow and wrongheaded analysis of ancient Mediterranean and Near Eastern texts (Jewish, Christian, and otherwise) that have long claimed to register the ideology of *contemptus mundi*. Too often the analysis renders those figured in the texts as being flat, uninteresting, apolitical, with narrow (that is, only anachronistically simple and flat) "religious" motives and interests (insofar as "religion" is overdetermined as belonging only to the private domain and having to do only with piety and ritual).

What should be looked for as part of the rhetorics and orientations of (African/African diaspora) *contemptus mundi* are the opportunities taken to tweak the regime, to critique it, to play with it, to signify on it, and to destabilize if not undermine it. All of this suggests again the importance of the concept of mimetics—with a difference. This "difference" is the "mimetic excess" about which Michael Taussig argues (following Horkheimer and Adorno) that breaks the normally violent repressed and closed circle of mimetics (the "simple" mimetics I discussed above). Combining "sensuousness with copy," mimetics of this sort reflects heightened or "reflexive awareness" so that as one acts one is aware of the acting, aware of the play, "as if" it were "real," as if "artifice" were "natural." Situated precisely—compellingly, necessarily?—in the situations of "postcoloniality," or post-slavery and Jim Crowism, in which the historically dispossessed and humiliated take hold of the tools and magical tricks that historically had been exclusively in the hands of the aboveground, the elites, including political-economic, intellectual, and religio-cultic virtuosi, this excess becomes a type of agency—a capacity "to live subjunctively" (that is, with the "freedom to live reality as really made-up").[62] Anything goes, Daniels came to understand, because everything was all made up.

It is this mimetic play—the engagement on an "as if" basis—that is a reflection of the rupture of meaning. Insofar as the dominant language regime operates on the basis of meaning—meaning-construction, meaning-seeking, meaning-maintenance—the rupture of meaning represents resistance or opposition, to be sure, but also what Douglass understood as his "glorious resurrection." This is how the silence, the nonparticipation is felt or experienced—in the freedom to recognize and act on the recognition that life is constriction and is to be lived "as if." This includes being *as if* dead. Thus, here is provided a blueprint for the *ongoing* experience of symbolic death.

I suggest that it is this orientation that Achebe, especially through his strong characterization of Obierika in *TFA*, at least opens the reader to imagine as a future possible. He challenges the reader not only to isolate and think about this thinking and orientation among the options, but also to build on, to develop and expand, it. Achebe addresses readers who, like him, as intellectual-activist in the mid-twentieth century, are oriented somewhat like Obierika—dreaming about, building and modeling through different means and types of efforts, a future for Umuofia-as-black Africa, defining themselves not so much in spite of the experience of things having fallen apart but thinking honestly and soberly and strategically and working through such a situation. What this points to is a history of efforts or histories of effort to define black existence in the modern world—in Africa and throughout the African diasporas—on the basis of a type of realistic *un*realism, an acknowledgment that things have indeed fallen apart (or whatever the linguistic or cultural-specific diaspora rendering of such a view might be).

The acknowledgment of things having fallen apart can serve as a touchstone and springboard for the pursuit of the complex structuring, rebuilding, and orientation of black life in the modern world that I identify in this chapter as *rupture of meaning*. As the complex, belated, reactive, ongoing part of the dynamics of human consciousness and conscientization called in this book scripturalectics, this turn in the dynamics of meaning-management represents a negotiation of the present challenges as well as the future possible that is emptied of, but at the same time made to confront and clash with, meaning as construction and regime. The clashes, performances, gestures, expressivities of *non*-meaning in reaction to the savagery of *hyper*-meaning can more broadly reflect and refract the nature of the contemporary world construction and strivings of the human. But this non-meaning as orientation is a rhetorical flourish, a necessary exaggeration. It is neither a flat nor a simple matter. It is not the same thing as emptiness, a void, indifference. It suggests a type of discipline—of playful non-engagement, a studied, willful refusal. It is layered and is/has a history.

Such a history I do not intend to relate in this book; it has been enough here to aim to isolate rupture in the dynamics of human-making. As part of an interest in seeking to know more about how meaning-management works, how it can be seen to have powerful, ambiguous effects and consequences, to have been worked in the past and to work still to flatten and enslave but also open up possibilities, we might begin looking rather broadly at different forms and types of expressiveness, forms and types that are not only resonant of rupture but also ever more complexly mimetic, ever more imitable, thereby opening ourselves to ways out and forward—from enslavement (to the frames of meaning) to marronage (of meaning).

I have in mind forms of expressiveness of the sort found in and carried by the works of contemporary artist Kara Walker. What her work provokes is the striking, even disturbing, recognition that some stories, some sentiments, some histories are made invisible or silent. By her own admission, Walker's works are shocking—"erotically explicit, shameless"—and were intended to provoke in the observer a sense of feeling "ashamed because they have . . . simply believed in the project of modernism." She is explicit about shaking loose the observer or critic from conventional modernist sensibilities and investment in history and meaning. She is, according to Kevin Young, "less an artist of history, whether racial or artistic history, than a historian of fantasy."[63]

In response to a particular exhibit of watercolor and graphite drawings entitled "Do You like Crème in Your Coffee and Chocolate in Your Milk," art critic Solange James registers a similar understanding of her exit from the house of meaning:

> Kara Walker's exhibition was a breath of fresh air—if it could be described as such. I was disgusted, embarrassed, and yet strangely intrigued, which illustrates the intensely paradoxical nature of her work and the issues that she seeks to bring attention to. She has no interest in creating a redemptive narrative for Blacks or Women. She is interested rather, in the continuity of conflict, for, as we know, nothing ever stands still. The fact that I found the fetishized images to be

both repulsive and titillating, speaks volumes to her power as an artist. Whether we like it or not, Ms. Walker shows us that we all, whether Black, White, Korean, Irish, Jewish, Male or Female, define ourselves based on some former master–slave dialectic, which we then in turn use to define ourselves. What protesting artists claim to be positive and empowering images of Blacks and Women, are in fact already contaminated mediums, as our consciousness is defined in opposition to an historical movement— whether that be slavery, ethnic segregation or woman's suffrage.[64]

Critic Phillippe Vergne argues that Walker's gesture of "cutting through" material and refashioning gesturing figures "cannot be an innocent one." There is in such gestures "violence"

> against the medium itself, as a maneuver to formalize her doubt when it comes to representation ... a blade directed against ... "those (stereo) typical targets ... hitting them off to the side ...to accentuate the negative space left by the archetypes' holes (silhouettes)."[65]

Such violence against form makes Walker's work a "*negative* space of representation, of all representations—an anti-image, a black hole. The *negative* space of representation ... may well swallow the dismissive trivializing way that black subjects have been represented in art history" (my emphases).[66] Her works are shocking, jolting, but they are not merely blunt. They do not mean in simple ways; they only "pretend" to follow the lines of a particular narrative, to create a certain expected or "reassuring" narratological effect. What they in fact produce is a "*fragmentation* of characters and anecdotal episodes that untie the knot of a storyline and undermine its ability to represent a common, shared history ... [w]hat ... can be termed 'disjunctive narratives.' "[67]

Walker's mural *Endless Conundrum* (Figure 3.1) is complexly about representation, and not just that of the antebellum South, or that of American history, but even more broadly that of Euro-American

Figure 3.1 Kara Walker, *Endless Conundrum, An African Anonymous Adventuress*, 2001.

Cut paper on wall
Approx. 191 × 453 inches (485.1 × 1150.6 cm)
Installation view:
Kara Walker: Mon Ennemi, Mon Frère, Mon Bourreau, Mon Amour
ARC/Musée d'Art moderne de la Ville de Paris, 2007
Photo: Florian Kleinefenn
Artwork: © Kara Walker, courtesy of Sikkema Jenkins & Co., New York.

modernity and its relation to the "primitive Other." *Endless Conundrum* has been considered the "family tree" of modernism, with Walker methodically and brilliantly "pruning" it.[68]

Utterly fascinating in *Endless Conundrum* is the figure of the colonizer, the master, in different scenes in the mural. How he is depicted is shocking and disturbing, to say the least. He is the master and the sculptor; his arms and one leg are locked to the black female figure he is "working on":

The sculpture being shaped as well as extracted, pleased as well as tortured, pushes him away with one hand and affectionately caresses his skull with the other, in a push–pull movement that conveys both

confusion and the horrible ambiguity of their sadomasochistic relationship in which one no longer knows who is kissing and who is being
kissed, who is eating and who is being eaten.[69]

Digestion, Vergne argues, might be the code word to make use of
when trying to make sense of *Endless Conundrum*. Digestion might
very well be what the crouching man at the top of the composition
is attempting as he molds a small sculpture while "defecating ...
'shitting' on 'them'—on the past, on authority, on hegemony, on violence, on history, on modernity, on power." "He is emancipating himself from all the muck—from Eurocentrism and all other repressive
'centrisms.'"[70]

Drawing on Oswald de Andrade's conceptual work on cultural
emancipation with focus on anthropophagy as a vital strategy in the
process of constituting autonomous language though appropriation,
Vergne is led to cannibalism (anthropophagy) as a wedge for understanding the "relation of otherness" and as a metaphor for violence.
It has to do with "the structuralization of societies, the birth of language or desire itself and the amorous fusion of individuals." Vergne
claims such notions strike at the heart of Walker's work. The latter is
a form of cannibalism: She is claimed to have "thoroughly swallowed
and digested codes of representations ... in order to elaborate her
own language."[71] Her work is seen as the equivalent of de Andrade's
manifesto: "Only anthropophagy unites us." As Vergne summarizes,
Walker's work is a "totem of taboos against all catechisms ... a radical demystification of religious, moral, political, and verbal power."[72]

With this glimpse at Walker's work as an example of the rupture
of history and meaning, with its focus on the fantastical as a path to
truth-telling, we should return to the colonial situation. The latter is
a reminder of the structure of relations that frame and determine and
set in motion the turns of scripturalectics that define human striving.
Walker's art reminds us just how universal and perduring is the situation in which Achebe's village of Umuofia finds itself. Yes, the "things"
into which we are born, into which we are educated and socialized,

onto which we are thrown, into which we are inscribed, these always in some form—by our own hands and efforts or by others' efforts—to some degree fall apart. What remains are our work and play—our daily, ongoing efforts in such situations at "living subjunctively," our self-reflexive mimetics and constructions of the fantastical for the sake of our finding agency and safe space. Things falling apart has to do mostly with loss of the levers of meaning. What remains after the falling apart are collective human efforts in dancing, marking, singing, drumbeating, horn-blowing, signifying, sculpting, loud talking, eating, cutting into and shitting on fixed truths and traditions—all as part of the response to the management of meaning as modern-world colonialist violence or savagery. Meaning in this vein—that is, *hyper*-meaning, *over*-managed meaning, the extreme or exaggerations required because of the constant need to police the peripherals and chronic strangers—is thereby being ruptured; and there is then the opportunity to make non-meaning—that is, to make meaning again not so much manageable, but now self-authorized and self-interested, thus, always fluid, a matter of healthy improvisation, free.

SUMMARY CONCLUSION

THE END OF SCRIPTURES, THE
BEGINNING OF SCRIPTURALECTICS

This book represents the unsettling of some widely shared assumptions, among them the following:

1. Scriptures have to do with specific isolable objects, a "there there" ("text"/"book").
2. "They" are projections from, about, and for a specific cordoned-off domain ("religion").
3. "They" represent and project this or that ("great" = worldwide) tradition (e.g., Christian, Jewish, Muslim, Hindu).
4. "They" are in our times believed in and prized (fetishized) only by a subset of demographics within this domain (religious zealots; white rubes who were not able to make of whiteness an advantage for them; and all those nonwhites who represent "the lag," the hyper-superstitious, noble savages, hyper-religious primitives of the world who with scriptures belatedly and slavishly mimic white men with their magic even as some white men move on to other tricks and games).
5. These fetishized objects must be engaged with an approved set of (academic or other field-specific professionally) prescribed/fetishized cultural practices (exegesis—from the level of primary-level catechetics to high academic scholarship, across fields).
6. Such practices ought normally be carried out with little or no political consciousness, intended interest, or consequence.

By coining the term and focusing on the analysis of *scripturalectics*, I have aimed in this book to explode such assumptions not so much by arguing the points with anyone but by modeling something quite different—a new trans-field and transdisciplinary critical analytical project in complex social-cultural formation, in the making and ongoing manipulation, enslavement, policing, agency, and freedom of the human. Using "scriptures"—the uses and turns in uses (-*lectics*) of an expansive and self-reflexive understanding of "scriptures" as discourse and power, as structures of communications and knowing—to think with, beyond any one current domain or field of studies, including religious/theological studies, construction of this new field of studies and area of research has been the pressing agenda. Here I make use of a phenomenon or problem or concept historically and at present that is mostly, with few exceptions, undertheorized, even collusively made impervious to theorizing, in religious/theological studies (and, frankly, in every other circle of discourse that references it). In this book I theorize it more broadly and radically. This theorizing places focus where, I have argued again and again, it should be: on the human, on how we are made and unmade in relationship to claims about knowledge and about discourse.

The different turns in knowledge claims and systems, in social relations, formations, and communications—the three major turns of scripturalectics—have served as a kind of wedge that forces reconsideration and disturbance of some of these long-held basic assumptions. First, with attention on scripturalization as language/discourse regime and policing, with scripturalism capturing the ideology of scripturalization, and with scripturalizing as a handle to describe ongoing mimetic practices and orientations in the making of difference, "religion," assumed as a cleanly separate domain from the "secular," which alone traffics in the scriptural, is made questionable. That scriptures are the (always) exclusive province/possession/portfolio of religion or any other single domain or type of authoritative figure is now challenged. Scriptures are to be considered as part of a framework for understanding relations and dynamics in every domain and sector of society. And the overdetermination of certain human groups or tribes as being particularly prone to the magic that scriptures are un/veiled to be must be turned on its head. It is "white men"—the Constantines and King Jameses and Antonin Scalias of history, symbolic and metonymic of the fabrications of "donations" (that is, of

authoritative, discursive policing figures and regimes of the world)—
who have invented and continue to invest in scriptures as part of their
"magic," their politics of meaning-management. They are the ones
who invent and make necessary meaning and its shape. Insofar as
the formerly enslaved, formerly colonized, minoritized, and subaltern
engage scriptures, they show themselves first to have been signified/
(en)scripturalized and then to have positioned themselves in complex
mimetic relationship to scripturalization, scripturalism, and scriptures
in order to position themselves for imaginative and discursive agency.
I have argued here that the minoritized in racial-ethnic and social-cultural terms are social-cultural-political canaries in the coalmine (or the
cave) and the always potential maroons leading us away from enslavement. To be clear, the subaltern—who are mostly peoples of color;
even more, mostly black peoples—should be especially important in
critical analysis of the scriptural, not because they deserve their political due in terms of attention or coverage, not because they have not
participated in their own local politics of meaning, but because they
were themselves the perceived necessary sites (at times in history quite
literally) on which and around which scripturalization as extensive
stable transcendence was constructed. Focus on the black ex-centrics'
experiences and expressivities—including their scripturalizing, as I
have tried to argue in this book—exposes, rents the veil/masking of
scripturalectics in all its turns. I have read Achebe's *TFA* as a particularly powerful window-opening project onto scripturalectics as I have
isolated some of its major turns.

Scriptures that are engaged not in the interest of reverberating
apologetic tribal theology but for the sake of critically addressing and
analyzing social formation must, I insist, be approached on the level
of the meta-textual. This level of engagement is necessary in order to
fathom *how* the textual is used. I cry again—to and for myself, for
my sanity and psychic health, mainly, but also to and for the sake
of other cultural-intellectual maroons—*it's scripturalization, stupid!*
Engagement of scriptures only on the text-object and theological/reli-
gious piety plane—no matter the self-location, no matter how dazzling
the methods and approaches—is obfuscation, mask-ing in the worst

sense, a meandering blind and deaf orientation in the arena of the "undiscussed" (Bourdieu), with the political significance—the uses—hidden to the benefit of the maintenance of the regimes of scripturalization. The substitution of text (what would Jesus do? whom did he marry?) for texture (what work, what set of interests or politics, is being pursued or pushed, with a scripturalized Muhammed or Buddha or Moses?) is mostly in the interest of management, in maintaining a type of ideological-political and psychosocial enslavement, the negative effects of ironic (gendered) "donations." That the exegetical play with text has sometimes been used for disentanglement from the clutches of meaning-management as slavery is the stuff of history. But such dynamics are the exception, requiring enormous ongoing (scripturalizing) work to effect and secure.

As Foucault challenged us to think about power, scriptures have no existence outside the type of social relations and psychosocial orientations I have tried to isolate here. That more turns in such relations and orientations may be isolated and probed I acknowledge, and I challenge readers to offer more research in this area, using other worlds to think with. I challenge readers to consider scriptures in terms of particular types of power relations and dynamics. There are no scriptures per se; there are only scripturalectics—social-political relations and psychosocial dynamics, and the human beings who invent and manage these dynamics or are managed by them.

So the critical study of the scriptural must now and henceforth be about social relations and dynamics, including the politics of language. The study of the scriptural in the highly interwoven twenty-first century and in terms of the quest for and realization of the highest forms and levels of freedom of thinking and agency must now not be delimited to the study of (the history or content-meaning or literary-rhetorical arrangements and styles of) texts—no matter the dazzling technique and approach and sensibility and solidarity expressed here and there. The text-reading agenda has been and is still locked into the colonial agenda of the politics of meaning as reading difference. Sometimes this means inventing difference for the sake of management or control or enslavement; at other times it means erasing difference and subsuming it into the politics of sameness. Scripturalism and scripturalization are my shorthand for the ideology and structures for these agenda.

No, the study of the scriptural must now be about how we engage each other—up close and personal, and across great distances; in cyberspace; sometimes deploying "texts" on terms established long ago, but always using discourse of some type and in some form to manage meaning. The study of the scriptural must be about excavation—of human beings registering discourse and power through whatever media are chosen and made available. So there are no scriptures—except, to speak of, that is, in terms of isolating, analyzing social relations, the politics of language, discourse and power. What we are enmeshed in, what we provoke and are determined by, is scripturalectics. For the sake of knowing and possessing ourselves and finding constructive and creative ways to engage others, we must learn to read the scripturalectics that we construct and project. That is, we must, as Sojourner Truth is reported to have said about her own practice, read not so much "letters," but "[wo] men and nations."

NOTES

INTRODUCTION

1. See the recently published collections of essays that I edited, *Refractions of the Scriptural: Critical Orientation as Transgression* (New York: Routledge, 2016), and *Scripturalizing the Human: The Written as the Political* (New York: Routledge, 2015), as efforts to advance the work being called for.

2. (New York: Oxford University Press). Hereafter, *WMM*.

3. Because I mean by it not so much the opposite, but more than what Henry Louis Gates means by it in his *Signifyin' Monkey*, I prefer this spelling. I do often follow him, as he follows vernacular traditions, in using "on," as in "signifying on" something or someone.

4. In the wake of the religious wars that marked European history before the early modern period, one might ask what other response might have been made. There is no need for me to resolve this issue here. I do need to note that the response comes with consequences with which we still grapple. Among them are the issues on which this book focuses.

5. See Pierre Bourdieu, *Outline of a Theory of Practice*, trans. Richard Nice (Cambridge, England: Cambridge University Press, 1977), 168.

6. On the semiosphere, see semiotician Yuri Lotman's voluminous writings, especially *Universe of the Mind: A Semiotic Theory of Culture*, trans. Ann Shukman (New York: I. B. Tauris, 2001). Another most helpful "translation" is Aleksei Semenenko's *The Texture of Culture: An Introduction to Yuri Lotman's Semiotic Theory* (New York: Palgrave Macmillan, 2012).

7. See Vincent Caretta's impressive edition of Equiano's story, *Olaudah Equiano: The Interesting Narrative and Other Writings*

(New York: Penguin Books, 2003), as well as his most comprehensive biographical work, *Equiano the African: Biography of a Self-Made Man* (Athens: University of Georgia Press, 2005).

8. Trans. Steven Rendall (3d ed.; Berkeley: University of California, 2011 [1980]).

9. I am here following Pierre Nora's terminology and conceptualization of a critical project and orientation, See his "Between Memory and History: Les Lieux de Mémoire," in *History and Memory in African-American Culture*, ed. Geneviève Fabre and Robert O'Meally (New York: Oxford University Press, 1994).

10. See her *Playing the Dark: Whiteness and the Literary Imagination* (New York: Vintage, 1991). Also see Satya P. Mohanty's *Literary Theory and the Claims of History: Postmodernism, Objectivity, Multicultural Politics* (Ithaca: Cornell University Press, 1997), which provides a persuasive argument for theorizing openly and honestly out of one's positionality and identity. More about this argument below.

11. See his *Significations: Signs, Symbols, and Images in the Interpretation of Religion* (Aurora, CO: The Davies Group, Publishers, 1999 [1986]), 4.

12. See *MisReading America: Scriptures and Difference*, ed. V. L. Wimbush (New York: Oxford University Press, 2013).

13. I conceptualized and organized an academic curricular program at Claremont Graduate University in 2008—and gave it this name. It is a program with which I am no longer involved or affiliated.

14. We are still a long way from a mature and broad-based critical discourse in this area, but there are hopeful signs and gestures, among which are the following: J. L. Matory's *Black Atlantic Religion: Tradition, Transnationalism and Matriarchy in the Afro-Brazilian Candomblé* (Princeton: Princeton University Press, 2005); Curtis J. Evans, *The Burden of Black Religion* (New York: Oxford University Press, 2008); and the relatively new *Journal of Africana Religions*.

15. Among recent examples, see *The Africana Bible: Reading Israel's Scriptures from Africa and the African Diaspora*, ed. Hugh Page, Jr., et al. (Minneapolis: Fortress, 2010); and *The New Testament: Fortress Commentary on the Bible*, ed. Margaret Aymer

et al. (Minneapolis: Fortress, 2014). T. Benny Liew, *What is Asian American Biblical Hermeneutics? Reading the New Testament* (Honolulu: University of Hawaii Press, 2008); *They Were All Together In One Place? Toward Minority Biblical Criticism,* ed. Randall C. Bailey et al. (Atlanta: Semeia Studies; Society of Biblical Literature, 2009); and *True to Our Native Land: An African American New Testament Commentary,* ed. Brian K. Blount et al. (Minneapolis: Fortress, 2007). It seems that no matter the special group identity politics and interests, no matter the sensibilities, methods and approaches, what remains in place is the baseline interest in the explication—the fetishization of—texts. The problem is the lack of problematization of this very phenomenon, this politics and set of practices, whence it comes, what psycho-social and political work it performs.

16. I consider my essay "The Bible and African Americans: An Outline of an Interpretative History" in *Stony the Road: African American Biblical Interpretation,* ed. Cain Hope Felder (Minneapolis: Fortress, 1991), to have been the first gesture, the opening salvo, in the direction of the critical project with which I am now associated and which has matured into the argument and orientation of this book.

17. See on this point the argument typically, that is to say, briefly and brilliantly posited, although not developed, by Krister Stendahl in his SBL Presidential address, "The Bible as a Classic and the Bible as Holy Scripture," in *Journal of Biblical Literature* 103:1 (March 1984): 9. Stability and dominance would seem to condition orientation to exegesis.

18. See Ishmael Reed, *Mumbo Jumbo* (New York: Scribner Paperback Fiction, 1972), and my take on it in relationship to politics of interpretation, especially for peoples of color, in "'We Will Make Our Own Future Text': An Alternate Orientation to Interpretation," in *True to Our Native Land: An African American New Testament Commentary,* ed. Brian K. Blount et al (Minneapolis: Fortress, 2007).

19. See from the theological/religious studies silo, Theophus Smith's *Conjuring Culture: Biblical Formations and Black America* (New York: Oxford University Press, 1994); Allan Callahan's *The*

Talking Book: African Americans and the Bible (New Haven: Yale University Press, 2008); and Michael Brown's *Blackening of the Bible: Aims of African Americans Biblical Scholarship* (Harrisburg: Bloomsbury T & T Clark, 2004). These projects address the situation in very different ways. Smith's training and orientation is theological and philosophical; Callahan offers what appears to be a cultural-historical approach and schema, addressing how different parts of the Bible are in evidence in different historical cultural settings; Brown is focused on the scholarly arguments and projects of individual scholars with little attention to larger social-cultural dynamics. From literary criticism, see Chanta Haywood, *Prophesying Daughters: Black Women Preachers and the Word, 1823–1913* (Columbia: University of Missouri Press, 2001); and Katherine Clay Bassard, *Transforming Scriptures: African American Women Writers and the Bible* (Athens: University of Georgia Press, 2011).

20. See on the topic Michael Taussig's provocative *Mimesis and Alterity: A Particular History of the Senses* (New York: Routledge, 1993). I consider him a fellow traveler and have drawn on him quite a bit in recent projects.

21. That is to say, in retrospect I judge that no bulbs were set off in terms of what might be considered a field-changing dissertation project. I simply demonstrated I had learned to play the (standard) field discourse game. This now seems to me to be a function of my not thinking and feeling that I was allowed to pursue in such a program the issues that roiled my gut. Without that roiling, sometimes understood as passion, there is only getting through it. Yet I am sometimes made to question this judgment of the situation: I can now see in the early work some gesturing and posturing, some faint cries on my part, in the direction I have since taken and owned: For example, although my dissertation topic and project appear to be fairly standard fare, I can see it in some first rumblings of interest in social-cultural formation, performativity, and orientation to the world.

22. Although this project had little or no impact on the curriculum at Union, several students there were energized by the project and became and remain collaborators.

23. (New York: Continuum International, 2000, 2001)

24. (Minneapolis: Fortress, 2003)
25. I was asked to consider writing this essay shortly after the AFAMBIB project and conference. There is no doubt that what the Stony the Road project and the book published in 1991 and the AFAMBIB project represented are now safe gambles, if not a bit of strategic exploitation in publishing corporations that had lines in religious/theological studies. These projects opened wide the door for works in this area. Fortress Press got on the bandwagon early on and never looked back. University presses soon followed. It was beginning to look like the fields would not be despoiled, the authors would not be run out of guilds with torches, books would be sold. Also important, if not much more so, peoples of color in the guilds were slowly during this period in the 1980s and 1990s beginning to accept as legitimate and compelling their work that made their identities visible. That this was not the case before this period I can attest. There were understandable palpable insecurities and anxiety and fear felt around the issue; scholarship had for so long been so defined and legitimized as invisible and silent discourses around whiteness that it could hardly have been otherwise.
26. See the novella in Richard Wright, *Eight Men: Short Stories* (New York: Harper Perennial Modern Classics, 2008).
27. (Durham: Duke University Press, 1999)
28. Following V. Caretta, I conclude that Equiano was likely born in South Carolina, with no direct knowledge of the practices or culture he described, but this does not mean the description is not rich and textured and reflective of verisimilitude. See Carretta's *Equiano the African*.
29. See the fascinating treatment of slavery in relationship to the development of the concept of consent in the (first and second) founding of the United States, in François Furstenberg, *In the Name of the Father: Washington's Legacy, Slavery, and the Making of a Nation* (New York: Penguin Books, 2006).
30. See Tony Bennett, "Texts, Readers, Reading Formations," in *The Bulletin of the Midwest Modern Language Association* 16:1 (Spring 1983): 3–17. I am influenced by this discussion but have developed the concept for my own interests in advancing the argument in the book.

31. Achebe's other novels—*No Longer at Ease* (1960), *Arrow of God* (1964), *A Man of the People* (1966), and *Anthills* (1987)—I considered integrating into the argument and discussion here, but they proved to be less compelling and workable than the focused reading and use of the one work, *TFA*, that also happens to be universally held as a classic and as his best novel. In TFA I found touchstones of the turns in scripturalectics that I needed for elaboration.

CHAPTER I

1. See her moving book, *Lose Your Mother: A Journey Along the Atlantic Slave Route* (New York: Farrar, Straus and Giroux, 2007).
2. And because of its complexity and layeredness, I shall not be able to resist making use of it again in the next chapter—for a different purpose of demonstration and argumentation, as another kind of example. Here I draw on it as springboard for discussion about this first turn in scripturalectics. See Jesuit missionary and ethnologist Joseph-François Lafitau's 1724 multivolume work *Moeurs des sauvages Amériquains comparées aux moeurs des premiers temps* (Paris: Saugrain l'aine at Charles Etienne Hochereau, 1724). Also: *Customs of the American Indians compared with the customs of primitive times*, trans. William Fenton and Elizabeth Moore (Toronto: Champlain Society, 1974).
3. See "Writing vs. Time: History and Anthropology in the Works of Lafitau," in *Rethinking History: Time, Myth, and Writing*, ed. Marie-Rose Logan and John Frederick Logan (Yale French Studies 59; New Haven: Yale University Press, 1989).
4. Long, *Significations*, 4. (See Introduction, n#11.)
5. I note here Achebe's own testimony about being directly provoked and outraged and challenged by Conrad's representation of black Africans in his *Heart of Darkness*. See his "An Image of Africa: Racism in Conrad's Heart of Darkness," in *Heart of Darkness: A Norton Critical Edition*, ed. Robert Kimbrough (New York: Norton, 1988), 251–262.
6. Recall Morrison's point, too riveting to comment on, in *Beloved* (New York: Penguin Books, 1987), 188–189:

Whitepeople believed that whatever the manners, under every dark skin was a jungle. Swift unnavigable waters, swinging screaming baboons, sleeping snakes, red gums ready for their sweet white blood. In a way, he thought, they were right. The more colored-people spent their strength trying to convince them how gentle they were, how clever and loving, how human, the more they used themselves up to persuade whites of something Negroes believed could not be questioned, the deeper and more tangled the jungle grew inside. But it wasn't the jungle blacks brought with them to this place from the other (livable) place. It was the jungle white-folks planted in them. And it grew. It spread. In, through and after life, it spread, until it invaded the whites who had made it. Touched them every one. Changed and altered them. Made them bloody, silly, worse than even they wanted to be, so scared were they of the jungle they had made. The screaming baboon lived under their own white skin; the red gums were their own.

7. Chinua Achebe, *Things Fall Apart: Authoritative Text, Contexts and Criticism*, ed. Francis Abiola Irele (New York: W. W. Norton & Company, 2009), 8. Hereafter *TFA*.

8. See with his argument about all human behavior as play Johan Huizinga, *Homo Ludens: A Study of the Play-Element in Culture* (Boston: Beacon Press, 1955 [1950]). This argument will be picked up and elaborated on by Robert N. Bellah, in his last and quite impressive book, *Religion in Human Evolution: From the Paleolithic to the Axial Age* (Cambridge: Harvard University Press, 2011). About the concept and the argument more below.

9. Although one should take note of Irele's note about gender as issue "running as an undercurrent to the narrative" (xvii). See also among the essays in the collection, Rhonda Cobham, "Problems of Gender and History in the Teaching of *Things Fall Apart*," 510–521.

10. Achebe records such attitudes and actions, like everything else that took place in that world, with what he became famous for—a chilling compression of words. His portrayal communicated the accepted naturalized ways of that world. Yet the brittle wording reflected—almost required seeing—cracks in the vessel, tears in the cultural cloth. The narrator forced readers to see that some deeply held traditions were falling apart.

11. Reference here to drum and flute inspired my research into such instruments and their functions in African and African diaspora traditions. The research in turn led me to apply to parts of the work of the Institute for Signifying Scriptures (ISS), which I founded and currently direct, names of instruments from these worlds—the *Abeng* and the *Gumbé*—that facilitated communications and formation work in African diaspora marronage. Go to signifyingscriptures.org.

12. See especially Irele's illuminating essay, "Cultural Memory in Things Fall Apart," 453–491, in particular 465, for perspective on the yam in the culture.

13. As Amiri Baraka would have it. See discussion in Kimberly W. Benston, *Performing Blackness: Enactments of African-American Modernism* (London and New York: Routledge, 2000), 13, 189–227.

14. From Zora Neale Hurston, *Mules and Men* (New York: Perennial Library, 1990 [1935]), 218

15. See on the matter of history richly conveyed by fiction Hayden White, *Tropics of Discourse Essays in Cultural Criticism* (Baltimore: The Johns Hopkins University Press, 1978), 89, 98, 121–123; and *Content of the Form: Narrative Discourse and Historical Representation* (Baltimore: The Johns Hopkins University Press, 1990), chaps 1–3.

16. His Chapter 3 is entitled "Tribal Religion: The Production of Meaning."

17. Bellah, 138–174.

18. Ibid., 129. He draws on several other theorists, including Huizinga, already referenced above, in describing the human as playing animal.

19. Ibid., 130.

20. Ibid., 134. My emphasis. Note how this argument complements M. Taussig's argument at end of *Mimesis and Alterity*, especially the idea of mimesis as "end in itself that takes one into the magical power of the signifier to act as if it were real ... [and] provides welcome opportunity to live subjunctively" (255). I tried to develop this argument in my Opening Address (" 'I Wish [We] Knew How it Would Feel to be Free': The Subjunctive Mood") at the Inaugural Annual Meeting of the Institute for Signifying Scriptures, Portland, Oregon, February 2016.

21. Bellah, 135. Here Bellah argues that James McClenon, *Wondrous Healing: Shamanism, Human Evolution, and the Origin of Religion* (DeKalb: Northern Illinois University Press, 2001), is too simplistic on the matter. But it is not clear to me what specifically is the bone he feels the need to pick with McClenon.

22. Bellah, 135. Quotation: Jonathan Z. Smith, *Imagining Religion: From Babylon to Jamestown* (Chicago: University of Chicago Press, 1982), 63. Emphasis in original.

23. Bellah, 136.

24. (Cambridge: Cambridge University Press, 1999). Before publication of Bellah's book I had over the years worked my way several times through Rappaport's dense and provocative book. I agree that it is an immensely engaging and compelling work.

25. My emphasis here: I can hardly fail to notice this poignant resonance with—almost direct quoting of—Achebe's title! Who's channeling whom in the discussion of these issues?!! Bellah, 135.

26. Rappaport, 24.

27. Bellah, 136. My emphasis.

28. Rappaport, 137–138.

29. Ibid., 39.

30. Ibid., 166.

31. Ibid., 255–256.

32. Ibid., 262.

33. Ibid., 263.

34. Ibid., 279, 309.

35. Ibid., 322f.

36. Ibid., 444.

37. Ibid., 429f.

38. Ibid., 444.

39. (New York: W. W. Norton and Company, 2001), 260.

40. Donald, 260f. See Chapters 7 and 8 for full discussion of different stages.

41. Ibid., 315.

42. Ibid., 321.

43. Ibid., 322–323.

44. (Bloomington and Indianapolis: Indiana University Press)

45. Goodman, 47.

46. Ibid., 47. To this matter I shall return below.
47. Ibid., 19.
48. Trans. Robert Bononno (Cambridge: Perseus Books)
49. Trans. Robert Bononno (Minneapolis: University of Minnesota Press)
50. Levy, *Collective Intelligence* (hereafter *CI*), 131f (Part II. The Knowledge Space.) I detect a channeling of Achebe's focus on place.
51. Ibid., 132.
52. Ibid., 134.
53. Ibid., 136.
54. Ibid., 137.
55. Ibid., 141.
56. (Washington: Smithsonian Institution Press and Manchester: Manchester University Press)
57. See especially his discussion (60f) of Alfred Gell's work (*Metamorphosis of the Cassowaries: Umeda Society, Language and Ritual* [London: Athlone Press, 1975]).
58. Werbner, 162.
59. Ibid., 155.
60. Ibid., 175.
61. Ibid.
62. Ibid., 176.
63. Ibid., 176, *pace* Gell. See Gell, 281.
64. Werbner, 182. See Victor Turner, *The Forest of Symbols: Aspects of Ndembu Ritual* (Ithaca: Cornell University Press, 1967), 93ff.
65. Werbner, 183.
66. I note here with some amusement and raised brow that this language ("as if") resonates with and draws me back to the interest that led to my focus in the writing of my dissertation (the still mysterious and not satisfactorily unexplained expression *hos me* in 1 Corinthians 7). See my *Paul the Worldly Ascetic: Response to the World and Self-Understanding According to 1 Corinthians 7* (Macon: Mercer University Press, 1987). Although I am still not yet sure what I was wrestling over, I have come to see it somewhat in line with, an interest in participating in, Taussig's discussion in *Mimesis and Alterity*, especially the focus on "living subjunctively." This connection is what I was alluding to in the Introduction (above) in the context of discussion about my academic-intellectual sojourn.

67. (Berkeley: University of California Press)
68. Napier, xxv.
69. Ibid., 3.
70. Ibid., 3–4.
71. Ibid., 15–16.
72. Ibid., 17.
73. Ibid., 18.
74. Ibid., 20–21.
75. We might think here of the ways in which, in our own fraught and tense times, police or civilian videos are managed/interpreted—by police, prosecutors, media, the public.
76. Note how Napier here, pp. 23–27, handles the matter of monotheism versus polytheism as different orientations.
77. Napier, 23.
78. Ibid., 24.
79. Ibid., 25.
80. Ibid., 25.
81. See my discussion in the Introduction and in *WMM*; and J. Lotman, *Universe of the Mind.*
82. See Jonathan A. Peters, *A Dance of Masks: Senghor, Achebe, Soyinka* (Washington, D.C.: Three Continents Press, 1978), for interesting comparative analysis.
83. Sam D. Gill, "Disenchantment," *Parabola: Myth and the Quest for Meaning* 1 (1976): 11. Quoted in Lawrence E. Sullivan, *Icanchu's Drum: An Orientation to Meaning in South American Religions* (New York: Macmillan Publishing Company, 1988), 337.

CHAPTER 2

1. A good place to begin fathoming the issue is with Claude Lévi-Strauss. See *Conversations with Claude Lévi-Strauss*, ed. G. Charbonnier, trans. John and Doreen Weightman (London: Jonathan Cape, Ltd., 1969), especially Chapter II (" 'Primitive' Peoples and 'Civilized' Peoples").
2. See on the phenomenon of certainty, Wendy James, ed., *The Pursuit of Certainty: Religious and Cultural Formation*s (London and

New York: Routledge, 1995), a fascinating collection of theory-sensitive essays.

3. But this only begs the question: How is it being used here? To be sure, there is here reflected a type of orientation and sensibility that suits the ideology of monotheism, with its roots in ancient worlds. See discussion in Chapter 1. But how this ideology is being deployed here, in this situation, is the issue, the point of this chapter.

4. Achebe is here channeling the myths of the noble savage and the Magical Negro as a subcategory.

5. On the related concept of "entextualization," see Webb Keane, *Christian Moderns: Freedom and Fetish in the Mission Encounter* (Berkeley: University of California Press, 2007), 14, 171, 261.

6. Achebe's angst as reflected in his novels would suggest that this is how he saw things.

7. See cursory discussion in Chapter 1.

8. See *The Writing of History*, trans. Tom Conley (New York: Columbia University Press, 1988 [1975]), 189–190, passim.

9. See Etienne Thuau, *Raison d'Etat et pensée politique à lépoque de Richelieu* (Paris: Editions Albin Michel, 2000), 169f. See also de Certeau, *Writing*, 155.

10. De Certeau, *Writing*, 155.

11. See Nicolas De La Mare, *Traité de La Police . . .* (Paris, 1722 [1705]), *Livre Second: De La Religion. Titre Premier: Que la Religion est le premier & le principal objet de la Police, & que dans tous les temps les soins en ont ete consiez aux deux Puissances, la spirituelle, & la temporelle.*

12. De Certeau, *Writing*, 187f; 189, n#131. This orientation throws different light on the scriptural politics that obtained among European nations, protestants versus Catholics, especially the British versus the French. The French, the Catholics generally, were not uninterested in the scriptural; they simply played a different style of scriptural politics from the protestants. All played the management game. It is worth noting that Equiano figured himself a proper protestant Englishman through his firm opposition to Father Vincent's supposed French Catholic biblical illiteracy. See *Interesting Narrative*, 200; *WMM*, 87–89.

13. For thick historical background and sharp analytical perspective on the project, what it reflected and set in motion, see Tomoko Matsuzawa, *The Invention of World Religions: Or, How European Universalism Was Preserved in the Language of Pluralism* (Chicago: University of Chicago Press, 2005), Chapter 7.

14. See Jonathan Z. Smith, *Imagining Religion* (Chicago: University of Chicago Press, 1982), xi.

15. Readers should note the recent flap at evangelical Wheaton College in Illinois over who is authorized to interpret Christian traditions and texts: apparently, not a black woman on the faculty, who arrogated to herself the right to be an interpreting agent of Christian faith. Dr. Larycia Hawkins and Wheaton, by "mutual agreement," parted ways. See *Chronicle of Higher Education* LXII:21(February 5, 2016): A23f.

16. Here I register my skepticism of Levy's claim that cyberculture represents a potential breakthrough of sorts in social relations and power dynamics. See his *Cyberculture*, trans. Robert Bononno ((Minneapolis: University of Minnesota Press, 2001 [1997]), Chapters 14–16.

17. See Marshall McLuhan, *The Gutenberg Galaxy: The Making of Typographic Man* (Toronto: University of Toronto Press, 1962).

18. (New York: W. W. Norton & Company, 2014). The project is distinguished, I supposed, by inclusion not of more traditions—the traditional (since Müller) "world" systems (6) are affirmed—but of more ("sectarian") texts *within* the established traditions. The framework is upheld and reinscribed.

19. (Boston: Beacon Press, 2000). See the comprehensive but also rather thrilling and compelling narration—openly and honestly in solidarity with non-elites—of the history of events and major and minor characters, racialist arguments and sentiments, forms of violence and resistance in this period. The book includes discussion about the development and translation of this biblical concept and others like it and what they mean in the discourses of the dominant Europeans.

20. Linebaugh and Rediker, 4.

21. In the discussion and argument about these matters I am following Linebaugh and Rediker, especially Chapters 2 and 3.

22. See his *Reflections on the Revolution in France* (1790), para. 133. And see Thomas Paine's response, in his *The Rights of Man* (1791).

23. There is much literature on color symbolization. I highly recommend Michael Pastoreau, *Black: History of a Color* (Princeton: Princeton University Press, 1999), a wide-ranging, very creative, multidisciplinary discussion.

24. Linebaugh and Rediker, 99. *Pilgrim's Progress*, Part One, Sect. IX.

25. Linebaugh and Rediker, 99. *Pilgrim's Progress*, Part Two, Sect. IX.

26. Ibid., Parts One and Two, Sect. IX.

27. Ibid. See online at: http://truthinheart.com/EarlyOberlinCD/CD/Bunyan/text/The.Holy.War/Entire.Book.html. Accessed March 29, 2016.

28. Linebaugh and Rediker on Bunyan: "[He] associates the African with the activities of the Ranters, or of his own youth ... here Bunyan blames the victim" (99).

29. See V. L. Wimbush, "Ascetic Behavior and Color-ful Language: Stories About Ethiopian Moses," *Semeia* 58 (Fall 1992): 81–91, for perspective on late ancient situation and example.

30. See edition by Roger Hayden (3d ed.; Bristol: Bristol Record Society, 1974). According to Linebaugh and Rediker, the records were first published first by E.D. Underhill in 1847. A second edition was published in 1865 by Nathaniel Haycroft, who, it is important to note, preserved much of the original orthography, paragraph divisions, capitalizations, and emphases. The preservation of the latter is especially important for interpretation. Linebaugh and Rediker include the entire passage that concerns sister Francis on pp. 73–74.

31. See the moving novel by Sherley Anne Williams, *Dessa Rose* (New York: Harper Perennial, 1999 [1986]), for a similar situation faced by a black female. The protagonist, a fiercely courageous slave woman who had been part of a slave revolt that resulted in the killing of several white men, escapes but is captured. Her execution is delayed on account of her pregnancy. While waiting she is interviewed by (the significantly named) Adam Nehemiah. Much poignancy turns around Nehemiah's interview questions and writing of a "record" of her testimony. Here is scripturalization up close. Ultimately, who inscribes whom? That such a question can be raised

suggests that scripturalization, like all regimes, provides possibilities for escape and being upended, even if only for a strategic moment.

32. Linebaugh and Rediker, 74. Bold emphasis in text source.

33. Linebaugh and Rediker, 73. It is thought that founder Dorothy Hazzard was the oral source.

34. And perhaps in a strange ironic twist also, if not more so, within this self-styled radical evangelical circle, striving in Terrill's time to become somewhat "mainline."

35. This interest in the use of scriptures within Francis's circle is of course what explains my focus on Equiano. It is interest in the historical development of such that has led me to commit to the writing of this book (and others to follow).

36. See Peter Fryer, *Staying Power: Black People in Britain since 1504* (Atlantic Highlands NJ: Humanities Press, 1984), for a comprehensive treatment.

37. White male is what must be assumed here. Royalty aside, with British socialization, who otherwise would be considered so? Given the means to purchase a sloop and command others to follow him in support of his initiatives, who but a white man can be assumed here? What follows in this episode makes that identity all the more significant.

38. Carretta, ed., *Olaudah Equiano*, n#563, re: Musquito Indians. He quotes Thomas Jefferys (*The West India Atlas* [1794]), who indicates that the British essentially exploited the "Miskito" peoples' hatred for the Spaniards who had conquered them and had driven their ancestors from their homeland near Lake Nicaragua. The British were opportunists, looking for ways to take advantage, in the usual respects, of this situation.

39. John Fox (1517–1587) was an English historian and martyrologist. His famous work lauds the courage and faith of Christian martyrs from the first century to the sixteenth century, focusing on the persecutions experienced by the English protestants of the sixteenth century and their forerunners from the fourteenth century through the reign of Mary I. There were many reprints in abridged editions, with woodcut illustrations in the eighteenth century. See Carretta, ed., *Olaudah Equiano*, n#563. Also, William Haller, *Foxe's First Book of Martyrs and the Elect Nation* (London: Jonathan Cape, 1963).

40. In what is modern-day Nicaragua and Honduras, off the Atlantic coast.

41. And, of course, its imbrication in mercantilism/emergent capitalism. See on the matter of Equiano's relationship to these phenomena, Houston A. Baker, Jr., *Blues, Ideology, and Afro-American Literature: A Vernacular Theory* (Chicago: University of Chicago Press, 1984), especially p. 31; and Joseph Fichtelberg, "World between Word: The Economy of Equiano's *Narrative*," *American Literary History* 5:3 (1993): 459–480.

42. I find it startling that this term that Equiano used is also used in one of the texts, written by Diego Méndez de Segura, regarding now-mythic events that took place during Columbus's fourth voyage: "*e yo di el ardid y la manera con que se debía hacer.*" See *The Four Voyages of Columbus: A History of Eight Documents, Including Five by Christopher Columbus, in the Original Spanish, with English Translations*, trans. and ed. Cecil Jane (New York: Dover Publications, Inc., 1988), 118–119. Diego Méndez de Segura sailed on the fourth voyage with Columbus as squire in the caravel *Santiago de Palos*, captained by Francisco de Porras. Not much more beyond the fact of his efforts to vindicate Columbus is known about him. See editor's note #2, p. 112. The use of the translated term "strategem" is suggestive: Might Equiano have taken his language directly from translation of this source? The other sources of this event do not use such language. Furthermore, *el ardid* (strategem, artifice, cunning) is suggestive of the "magic" of the white men that Equiano aimed to surface and play with.

43. I'll not here provide historical background on the Columbus story. I direct the reader to my discussion in *WMM*, 159f.

44. See Chapter 2, n#7.

45. See *The Life of the Admiral Christopher Columbus By His Son Ferdinand,* trans. and annotated by Benjamin Keen (New Brunswick: Rutgers University Press, 1959).

46. See *Short Account of the Destruction of the Indies*, trans. Nigel Griffin (London: Penguin, 1999).

47. *Four Voyages*, 134.

48. *Life of the Admiral*, 272–273.

49. I refer readers to useful discussions in Michel Foucault, *Power/ Knowledge: Selected Interviews and Other Writings, 1972– 1977*, ed. and trans. Colin Gordon (New York: Pantheon Books, 1980); and Michael Mann, *Sources of Social Power, vol. 1* (New York: Cambridge University Press, 1986), as starting points.

50. See *Interesting Narrative*, 52, 55, 57, 58, 59, 62–69, 77–78.

51. See Carla Gardina Pestana, *Protestant Empire: Religion and the Making of the British Atlantic World* (Philadelphia: University of Pennsylvania Press, 2009), Chapters 5–7; Linda Colley, *Britons: Forging the Nation, 1707–1837* (New Haven: Yale University Press, 1992); William R. Hutchison and Hartmut Lehmann, eds., *Many Are Chosen: Divine Election and Western Nationalisms* (Minneapolis: Fortress, 1994); David W. Kling, *The Bible in History: How the Texts Shaped the Times* (New York: Oxford University Press, 2004), Chapters 2, 4, 5; and Christopher Hill, *The English Bible and the 17th-Century Revolution* (UK: Penguin Books, 1993), Introduction and Chapters 10 and 11.

52. See for a comprehensive discussion about developments in sixteenth- and seventeenth-century England, Keith Thomas, *Religion and the Decline of Magic* (New York: Scribner 1971), Chapters 7–9, 14–17, 19, 20.

53. Those preserving and advancing the myth of Columbus do not use a specific term at all in reference to Columbus's power. It is as though it was important to keep secret or certainly mystifying even the concept by which what was being done was done. The Columbus myth is a fascinating example of the formation of a modern hero cult. This includes his own writings, in addition to the clearly vindicationist apologetic writings of others. Beyond that, a cult developed that any can hardly deny obtains in the present throughout the North Atlantic worlds. In his mimetics in relationship to Columbus, Equiano seemed to be very much tuned in to, or an apt reader of, large dynamic trends.

54. It might be helpful to investigate the modern American fantasy of the Wizard of Oz, especially the depiction of the wizard, in relationship to the "magic" that Equiano encounters. The one may illuminate the other. See for critical perspectives Ranjit S. Dighe, ed., *The Historian's Wizard of Oz: Reading L. Frank Baum's Classic*

as a Philosophical and Monetary Allegory (Westport, CT: Praeger, 2002); Paul Nathanson, Over the Rainbow: The Wizard of Oz as a Secular Myth of America (Albany: SUNY Press, 1991); and Evan I. Schwartz, Finding Oz: How L. Frank Baum Discovered the Great American Story (Boston: Houghton Mifflin, 2009).

55. On this point see Mary Louise Pratt, Imperial Eyes: Travel Writing and Transculturation (New York: Routledge, 2008), Part III; "Scratches on the face of the country; or, what Mr. Burrow saw in the land of the Bushmen," in Henry Louis Gates, Jr., ed. "Race," Writing, and Difference (Chicago: University of Chicago Press, 1986); and Apocalypse in the Andes: Contact Zones and the Struggle for Interpretive Power (Washington, D.C.: IDB Cultural Center, 1996); Jean and John Camaroff, Of Revelation and Revolution: Christianity, Colonialism, and Consciousness in South Africa, vol. 1 (Chicago: University of Chicago Press, 1991), Chapters 3, 5, 7; David Chidester, Savage Systems: Colonialism and Comparative Religion in Southern Africa (Charlottesville: University Press of Virginia, 1996), Chapters 1–3.

56. (London: Orbis Publishing Ltd., 1979)

57. Blackburn, 36. "Slightly adapted" from W. Lloyd Warner, A Black Civilization: A Social Study of an Australian Tribe (New York: Harper & Row, 1937 and 1965).

58. Blackburn, 55.

59. See, for starters, Philip Jenkins, New Faces of Christianity: Believing the Bible in the Global South (New York: Oxford University Press, 2006); The Bible in Africa, ed. Gerald O. West and Musa W. Dube (Leiden: Brill Academic Publication, 1998); R. S. Sugirtharajah, The Bible and Asia: From the Pre-Christian Era to the Postcolonial Age (Cambridge: Harvard University Press, 2013).

60. See Rosamond C. Rodman's "'We are Anglicans, They Are the Church of England': Uses of Scripture in the Anglican Crisis," in James S. Bielo, ed., The Social Life of Scriptures: Cross-Cultural Perspectives on Biblicism, ed. James S. Bielo (Signifying [on] Scriptures Series; New Brunswick: Rutgers University Press, 2009), 100–113, for very helpful historical and analytical perspective on this phenomenon. Also, in order to see just how fraught and ironic the situation continues to be, one should take note of the near

paralysis, certainly stuttering, on the part of the recently elevated primate of the U.S. Episcopal Church—an African American—as he attempts to respond to questions about how the issues have been roiling the Anglican Communion worldwide, especially the relationship between the contemporary U.S. and African Anglicans. See "Episcopal Church's First Black Leader, a Gay Marriage Backer, Focuses on Race," *New York Times*, March 18, 2016: http://www.nytimes.com/2016/03/19/us/episcopal-church-michael-curry-gay-marriage-racial-justice.html?_r=0. Accessed March 29, 2016.

CHAPTER 3

1. See my earlier brief reference in Introduction n#31 about Achebe's other novels and their interrelationships. It has been noted that Achebe intended to write a type of historical fictional series. More discussion below.

2. See Abdul R. JanMohamed, *The Death-Bound-Subject: Richard Wright's Archaeology of Death* (Durham: Duke University Press, 2005), 289. This is a very rich and arresting and disturbing book. JanMohamed is influenced by Judith Butler (*The Psychic Life of Power: Theories in Subjection* [Stanford: Stanford University Press, 1997]) in arguing, using Richard Wright's work to think with, that "the only form of 'power' made available to the death-bound-subject by the master consists of using his agency to bind himself further through the affective equivalents of his own bodily fluids, to his own condition as a death-bound-subject." What "affective equivalents of ... bodily fluids" may refer to is not entirely clear. But might there be some relationship to mimetics?

3. He took his book title and epigraph from W. B. Yeats's "The Second Coming."

4. This argument approaches from a different direction but is not far from what Paul Gilroy argues in *The Black Atlantic: Modernity and Double Consciousness* (London: Verso, 1993).

5. See on this subject the fascinating discussion by Susan Buck-Morss, *Hegel, Haiti, and Universal History* (Pittsburgh: University of Pittsburgh Press, 2009).

6. See my essays: "*Contemptus Mundi*: The Power of an Ancient Rhetorics and Worldview," *Union Seminary Quarterly Review* 47:1–2 (1994): 1–13; and "*Contemptus Mundi* Means '. . . Bound for the Promised Land . . .': Religion from the Site of Cultural Marronage," in *The Papers of the Henry Luce III Fellows in Theology*, vol. 2, ed. Jonathan Strom (Atlanta: Scholars Press, 1997), 131–161.

7. See two important primary texts—Bernard of Cluny, *Scorn for the World: Bernard of Cluny's "De Contemptus Mundi,"* ed. Ronald E. Pepin (Medieval Texts and Studies No. 8; East Lansing MI: Colleagues Press, 1991); and Lothario Dei Segni (Pope Innocent III), *On the Misery of the Human Condition [De miseria humane conditionis]*, ed. Donald R. Howard (Library of Liberal Arts No. 132; New York: Bobbs-Merrill Company, Inc., 1969). And see discussion in Jean Delumeau, *Sin and Fear: The Emergence of Western Guilt Culture: 13th–18th Centuries* (New York: St. Martin's Press, 1990); and in Ann Ramsey, "Flagellation and the French Counter-Reformation: Asceticism, Social Discipline and Evolution of a Penitential Culture," *Asceticism*, ed. Vincent L. Wimbush and Richard Valantasis (New York: Oxford University Press, 1995, 2002), 576–587.

8. On this subject, it is best to begin with S. Eisenstadt, ed., *Origins and Diversity of Axial Age Civilizations* (Albany: SUNY Press, 1986).

9. See Houston A. Baker, Jr., *Modernism and the Harlem Renaissance* (Chicago: University of Chicago Press, 1984), for a provocative resignification argument. See also the more recently published book by, Neil Roberts, *Freedom as Marronage* (Chicago: University of Chicago, 2015) which, as I understand it, has similar argumentation. I was unfortunately not able to enter into conversation with this book. For perspectives on the larger comparative historical background, see the collection of essays edited by Richard Price, *Maroon Societies: Rebel Slave Communities in the Americas* (Baltimore: Johns Hopkins University Press, 1996 [1973]); John Hope Franklin and Loren Schweninger, *Runaway Slaves: Rebels on the Plantation* (New York: Oxford University Press, 1999); and, of course, J. G. Stedman's *Narrative of a Five-Years' Expedition, Against the Revolted Negroes of Surinam in Guiana . . . 1772, to 1777* (London: J. Johnson and J. Edwards, 1796).

10. Not in chronological order: This sort of issue or problem does not easily lend itself to neat historical-developmental schemas. Such neatness or schema would, given my larger argument in this chapter, be ironic, if not an undermining effort.

11. http://www.allmusic.com/song/people-make-the-world-go-round-mt0005779807. Accessed March 17, 2016.

12. Of course, Isabel Wilkerson's phenomenal book *The Warmth of Other Suns: The Epic Story of America's Great* Migration (New York: Vintage, 2011) comes to mind here. More discussion of her below.

13. Included in *The Oxford Frederick Douglass Reader*, ed. William L. Andrews (New York: Oxford University Press, 1996). References below, cited as *Narrative*, are from this edition.

14. What follows is a slightly revised interpretation of this source-text that is found in my Society of Biblical Literature Presidential Address, "Interpreters—Enslaving/Enslaved/Runagate," *Journal of Biblical Literature* 130:1 (Spring 2011): 5–24.

15. The poignancy of such an issue for Douglass can be seen in the fact that at that point in Douglass's career William Lloyd Garrison and other white abolitionists sought to hover over and determine Douglass as writer. Garrison provided the preface to Douglass's 1845 *Narrative*. Whatever may be said about the substantive comments made in it, it is clear that this preface functioned primarily to "translate" Douglass—that is, to provide the meta-commentary for all that is to follow. This is an example of enslavement as a kind of "framework." A discerning reader can determine whether Garrison ever really understood Douglass's text. Douglass later severed ties with Garrison and the Garrisonians. He came to understand how slavery could continue to work—way up North—as discursive framing. On Garrison's persistent paternalism in relationship to Douglass, see Houston A. Baker, Jr., *The Journey Back: Issues in Black Literature and Criticism* (Chicago: University of Chicago Press, 1984), 148–149.

16. *Narrative*, 27–38.

17. This is the title of Ishmael Reed's most famous and challenging and sometimes unfathomable novel (New York: Scribner, 1972). For his purposes, Reed traced "mumbo jumbo" to Mandingo

ma-ma-gyo-mbo, a "magician who makes the troubled spirits go away" (7). This tracing suggest that which has meaning within a larger structure of meaning. Obviously, in the hyperracialized West that defines itself over against the black presence, the works and discourses of such a "magician" would be translated as nonsense, so much jumbled mumbling, a channeling of the "unmeaning jargon" that Douglass references.

18. Benston, 293.

19. For a fascinating exploration of this term and the phenomenon to which it points see literary and cultural critic Houston A. Baker, Jr., *Blues, Ideology, and Afro-American Literature: A Vernacular Theory* (Chicago: University of Chicago Press, 1984), 155, and passim.

20. See it in *The Collected Poems of Robert Penn Warren* (Baton Rouge: LSU Press, 1998), 39–40.

21. See this argument developed by Frantz Fanon in his *Wretched of the Earth,* trans. Constance Farrington (New York: Grove Press [1961] 1968), 41. Also see discussion in Abdul R. JanMohamed, "The Economy of Manichean Allegory: The Function of Racial Difference in Colonialist," in *Critical Inquiry* 12 (Autumn 1985): 59–87.

22. See the compelling development of this concept by Shankar Vedantam in *The Hidden Brain: How Our Unconscious Minds Elect Presidents, Control Markets, Wage Wars, and Save our Lives* (New York: Spiegel & Grau, 2010).

23. See his *Notes on the State of Virginia,* ed. with Introduction and Notes by Frank Shuffelton (New York: Penguin Books, [1785] 1999), 147.

24. Susan Buck-Morss, *Hegel, Haiti and Universal History,* and Sibylle Fischer, *Modernity Disavowed: Haiti and the Cultures of Slavery in the Age of Revolution* (Durham and London: Duke University Press, 2004), advance compelling arguments about Hegel's denial of the implications of the Haitians' struggle to be free and to establish the first modern society with aspirations to universal nonracialized freedoms.

25. For general historical-cultural background, focusing mainly on Britain, see Olivia Smith, *The Politics of Language, 1791–1819* (Oxford: Clarendon Press, 1984). For a discussion of John Locke

and the dramatic consequences in many domains and contexts in the twenty-first century in the United States, see Richard Bauman and Charles L. Briggs, *Voices of Modernity: Language Ideologies and the Politics of Inequality* (New York: Cambridge University Press, 2003), passim.

26. See http://archives.cnn.com/TRANSCRIPTS/0803/14/acd.01.html.

27. See Camara Jules P. Harrell, *Manichean Psychology: Racism and the Minds of People of African Descent* (Washington, D.C.: Howard University Press, 1999), for discussion of the way black peoples have been infected.

28. On this point there are so many possibilities for extending consideration and conversation. I like very much the way Christopher L. Miller, *Blank Darkness: Africanist Discourse in French* (Chicago: University of Chicago Press, 1985), 246, movingly sums up the matter: "One can assert with assurance that the relationship between Europe and Africa has continually been represented as simply North over South, light over dark, white over black: as an unmediated pairing of opposites. As discourse dependent on such a polarized logic has a hard time saying what it means, and it bears a perverse relation to the truth."

29. Already referenced above.

30. See de Certeau, Part IV, Chap X.

31. The language of Edmund Burke, found in his *Reflections on the Revolution in France, And on the Proceedings in Certain Societies in London Relative to that Event. In a Letter Intended to Have Been Sent to a Gentleman in Paris* (1790). It provoked much reaction in England and beyond. See also Smith, *Politics of Language*, Chapter III.

32. On this matter of canonical or conventional discourses, see Grey Gundaker, *Signs of Diaspora, Diaspora of Signs: Literacies, Creolization, and Vernacular Practice in African America* (New York: Oxford University Press, 1998). For a more conventional history of conventional literacy among blacks, see Janet Duitsman Cornelius, *"When I Can Read My Title Clear": Literacy, Slavery, and Religion in the Antebellum South* (Columbia: University of South Carolina Press, 1992).

33. See David Van Leer, "Reading Slavery: the Anxiety of Ethnicity in Douglass's Narrative," in *Frederick Douglass: New Literary*

and Historical Essays, ed. Eric Sundquist (New York: Cambridge University Press, 1990) 129.

34. See Orlando Patterson's works on slavery and freedom: *Freedom* (New York: Basic Books, 1991); *Slavery and Social Death: A Comparative Study* (Cambridge: Harvard University Press, 1982); and *Rituals of Blood* (Washington, D.C.: Civitas, 1998), among others.

35. Ann Kibbey and Michele Stepto, "The Anti-Language of Slavery: Frederick Douglass's 1845 *Narrative,*" in *Critical Essays on Frederick Douglass,* ed. William L. Andrews (Boston: G. K. Hall & Co., 1991).

36. Ralph Ellison, *Invisible Man* (2nd ed.; New York: Vintage, 1995), 3.

37. See Ta-Nehesi Coates's recent book *Between the World and Me* (New York: Spiegel & Grau, 2015) about the treatment of the black body as the motoring of "American" history and tradition, and the silence about it. As for historical examples of the silencing, I make reference to Rebecca Protten, an eighteenth-century pioneer Moravian missionary and evangelist and founder of one of the first African American protestant congregations in the North Atlantic world. See Jon F. Sensbach, *Rebecca's Revival: Creating Black Christianity in the Atlantic World* (Cambridge: Harvard University Press, 2005), for the story. The establishment politics of "church"/"religious" history has contributed to her being largely forgotten. I have already made reference to the woman known as "sister Francis" or as the "Blackymore maide." Her well-known charismatic leadership in the establishment of the seventeenth-century radical protestant formation that became the establishment Church of Christ in Broadmead, later Broadmead Baptist Church, Bristol, England, was erased by Edward Terrill's establishmentarian revisionist history. Her leadership was reduced to overdetermined categories—of appellation and sentimentality. She was by exegetical sleight of hand erased out of her rightful place in history, as founding figure, and then flattened into a black pious maid. See Edward Terrill, *Record of a Church of Christ in Bristol, 1640–1687.*

38. From "IX. Of the Sons of Master and Man," *Souls,* 114.

39. See Jean Fouchard, *The Haitian Maroons: Liberty or Death,* trans. A Faulkner Watts (New York: Edward Blyden Press, 1981); Alvin O.

Thompson, *Flight to Freedom: African Runaways and Maroons in the Americas* (Kingston, Jamaica: University of West Indies Press, 2006); Hugo Prosper Learning, *Hidden Americans: Maroons of Virginia and the Carolinas* (New York: Garland Publishing, 1995); Mavis Christin Campbell, *The Maroons of Jamaica, 1655–1796: A History of Resistance, Collaboration & Betrayal* (Granby, MA: Bergin & Garvey, 1988); Richard Price, ed., *Maroon Societies: Rebel Slave Communities in the Americas* (Baltimore: Johns Hopkins University Press, [1973] 1996); John Hope Franklin and Loren Schweninger, *Runaway Slaves: Rebels on the Plantation* (New York: Oxford University Press, 1999); and, of course, J. G. Stedman's *Narrative of a Five-Years' Expedition, Against the Revolted Negroes of Surinam in Guiana ... 1772, to 1777* (London: J. Johnson and J. Edwards, 1796). As already indicated, The recently published book by Neil Roberts, *Freedom as Maronnage*, I was unfortunately not able to engage before completing this book.

40. (New York: Touchstone, 1999), 6.

41. Wilkerson, 536. Note in her epigraph the use of Richard Wright. About him more below.

42. See Douglas A. Blackmon, *Slavery By Another Name: The Re-Enslavement of Black Americans from the Civil War to World War II* (New York: Anchor, 2008). A depressingly honest book.

43. See Michael Holland, ed., *The Blanchot Reader* (London: Blackwell, 1995), especially regarding the concept of "the work."

44. *Souls*, 3.

45. Of course, the debate about what this means or when and how this was experienced and what should be the response to it rages on. Although it was not Du Bois's proposed analysis of or proposed solution to the problem, many critics of black existence have argued that enslavement has meant above all alienation to the point of the loss of a ("sense of") past and that only the future remained as a basis for organization and orientation. For an informative discussion see Frank M. Kirkland, "Modernity and Intellectual Life in Black," *Philosophical Forum*, xxi:1–3 (Fall–Spring 1992–93); and Orlando Patterson, "Toward a Future That Has No Past: Reflections on the Fate of Blacks in the Americas," in *The Public Interest* 27 (Spring 1972).

46. *Narrative*, 69.
47. JanMohamed, *Death-Bound-Subject*, 17, 298–299.
48. I note here again the connection Wilkerson makes to Richard Wright with the epigraph of her book.
49. JanMohamed, *Death-Bound-Subject*, 303, n#15.
50. In *Eight Men: Short Stories by Richard Wright* (New York: HarperPerennial, 2008), 19–84. References from this source edition.
51. Perhaps, some have thought, in homage to Frederick Douglass.
52. Robert Hayden, "Runagate, Runagate," *Norton Anthology*, 1506–1508.
53. Carla Cappetti, "Black Orpheus: Richard Wright's 'The Man Who Lived Underground,'" *MELUS* 26:4 (Winter 2001), 41–68, especially 43, 47.
54. *Souls*, 183.
55. *Afro-American Poetics: Revisions of Harlem and the Black Aesthetic* (Madison: University of Wisconsin Press, 1988), 88–110.
56. Ibid., 106. See also Susan Sontag, "The Aesthetics of Silence," in *A Susan Sontag Reader* (New York: Vantage, 1983), 181–204.
57. (Chicago: University of Chicago Press, 1987), see Chapter 8.
58. Morrison, *Beloved*, 248.
59. See Buck-Morss's *Hegel, Haiti, and Universal History* (Pittsburgh: University of Pittsburgh Press, 2009), 127, n#112; and Dayan's *Haiti, History, and the Gods* (Berkeley: University of California Press, 1998), 35–37.
60. Baker, "Lowground and Inaudible Valleys," 106.
61. *Souls*, 179, 180, 182, 186.
62. Taussig, 254–255.
63. http://www.autostraddle.com/artist-attack-kara-walker-blends-history-with-fantasy-makes-you-fantastically-uncomfortable-133588/. Accessed March 28, 2016.
64. Art Critique: Kara Walker, http://copiousmagazine.com/08_summer/art+photography/kara_walker.html. Accessed February 26, 2016.
65. See Philippe Vergne, "The Black Saint Is the Sinner Lady," in *Kara Walker: My Complement, My Enemy, My Oppressor, My Love*, org. Philippe Vergne (Minneapolis: Walker Art Center, 2007), 14.
66. Ibid.

67. Ibid., 17.
68. Ibid., 17–18.
69. Ibid., 22.
70. Ibid.
71. Ibid., 22–23.
72. Ibid., 23.

INDEX

abjection, reflexive circuit of, 108, 175n2.
  See also JanMohamed
Achebe, Chinua, x, 22, 23, 30, 31, 33, 34,
  51, 59, 64, 65, 67, 69, 70, 72, 76, 79,
  81, 101, 106, 110–114, 116, 117, 118,
  132, 134, 149
Africa, dark, 31
African Americans and the Bible Research
  Project (AFAMBIB), 14, 15, 17. *See
  also* Wimbush
*African Americans and the Bible: Sacred
  Texts and Social Textures*, 16. *See also*
  Wimbush
alternate reality, 47, 48
anti-language, 126
Aravamudan, Srinivas
  (*Tropicopolitans*), 17
archaeology of death, 132. *See also*
  JanMohamed
el ardid, 172n42. *See also* stratagem
Aru oyim de de de dei, 25, 27, 35.
  See also *TFA*

Baker, Houston, Jr., 116, 122, 141
Bearden, Romare, 116
Bellah, Robert N., 38, 39, 40, 42
Berlin Conference, 72
The Bible and African Americans, 16.
  See also Wimbush
black (w)hole, 122. *See also* Henderson
Blackburn, Julia, 98
Blackymore Maide, 82

Blanchot, Maurice, 129
Buck-Morss, Susan, 141
Bunyan, John, 80–85

cargo, 89, 101
Columbus, Christopher, 89–90, 92–93,
  95–97, 101
Columbus, Ferdinand, 91
Conrad, Joseph, 30, 31
contemptus mundi, 115, 116, 128, 142–143
critical comparative scriptures, 6. *See also*
  Wimbush
critical history/critical historical, 4
Croon, J. H., and F. Alheim, 56
cybernetics of the holy, 41

dancing, 60
De Certeau, Michel, 3, 28, 71
De la Mare, Nicolas, 71
De las Casas, Bartolomé, 90
dialectics of death, 132. *See also*
  Jan Mohamed
Diego Méndez de Segura, 90
dividé et impera. See Müller
Donald, Merlin, 43–46
Douglass, Frederick (*Narrative*), 119, 120,
  124, 126, 129–131, 133
source for isolation of types of
  consciousness, 131–133
Du Bois, W. E. B. (*Souls of Black Folk*),
  10, 14, 124, 126, 130, 141
Dyan, Joan, 141–142